Research
Interviewing

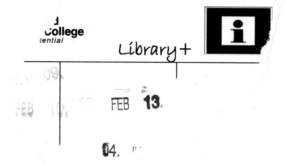

Research Interviewing

The range of techniques

Bill Gillham

Open University Press

Open University Press
McGraw-Hill Education
McGraw-Hill House
Shoppenhangers Road
Maidenhead
Berkshire
England
SL6 2QL

e-mail: enquiries@openup.co.uk
world wide web: www.openup.co.uk

and

Two Penn Plaza,
New York, NY 10121-2289, USA

First Published 2005
Reprinted 2007

A catalogue record of this book is available from the British Library

ISBN-10: 0335 21586 6 (pb) 0355 21587 4 (hb)
ISBN-13: 978 0 335 21586 7 (pb) 978 0 335 21587 4 (hb)

Library of Congress Cataloging-in-Publication Data
CIP data applied for

Typeset by RefineCatch Limited, Bungay, Suffolk
Printed in UK by Bell & Bain Ltd., Glasgow

Contents

Preface

This is a practical guide and it has been an intellectually challenging one to write – reflecting the challenge of teaching and supervising able postgraduate students in a range of settings. The approach taken is rooted in the conviction that the outcomes of research, empirical and theoretical, are only as good as the methods and procedures that underpin them. I would echo Lord Kelvin's observation that he never really trusted a theory until he could make a working model of it; in social research it is the operational detail of *methods* of investigation that test attractive theories.

Or as a student said to me, many years ago: *Very interesting: how exactly would you do that?*

Bill Gillham

Acknowledgements

Sarah Lowndes, PhD student in the Glasgow School of Art, has written Chapter 15 on e-mail interviewing: one of several areas where she is competent and I am not. She also reviewed a late draft of the entire manuscript.

My colleague Raid Hanna has applied his specialized intelligence to a review of Chapter 20 dealing with quantitative methods.

As always, my wife Judith has greatly improved the clarity of the writing by identifying jargon, redundancy and obscurity; and intellectual self-indulgence.

Clare Cannon has worked tirelessly to produce the finished transcript, starting with the unenviable task of translating my handwriting.

A more general debt is due to the research students in the School of Design at the Glasgow School of Art for their unrelenting demands that I explain methods clearly in practical terms and justify their use. Meeting their requirements has helped me extend the boundaries of conventional methods and these are evidenced in the text: in particular, I would mention Chris Lim's research into inclusive product design.

Finally, I want to acknowledge an intellectual debt to the contributors to *Qualitative Interviewing with Text, Image and Sound* (2000) edited by M. W. Bauer and G. Gaskell, the most original book in this area for some time; not least because it clarified my thinking where I found myself in disagreement.

The responsibility for any errors, infelicities or other limitations that remain can be placed firmly with the author.

Figures

Tables

Accustom yourself to give careful attention to what others are saying, and try your best to enter into the mind of the speaker.

Marcus Aurelius
Meditations

PART I
Principles and Practice

1 Research interviewing: key issues

The motivation for the present book comes from practical experience of the needs of postgraduate research students and others doing research in 'real-world' contexts who need to identify interviewing methods appropriate to their topic. There is more than one way of carrying out an interview, some more costly in terms of time and resources; and all of them more so than the universally popular questionnaire. In the main, interviews and questionnaires serve different purposes: to carry out a large-scale or preliminary survey you use questionnaires; to achieve a depth of understanding, you use an appropriate form of interview.

Interviews are inherently more flexible, whatever the level of structure, ranging as they do from 'listening in' and asking questions in a real-life setting to the standardized recording schedules used by market researchers. Questionnaires are difficult to do well and easy to do badly (Gillham 2000a: 1). In the latter case the data are worthless, and in the former they tend to be superficial but can point to further 'in-depth' research. Only limited inferences can be made because you cannot explore what lies behind the answers to the questions.

How is an interview to be defined? Not all of the variety of interviews described in this book meet all of the following criteria, but these are the main features:

1 Questions asked, or topics raised, are 'open' with the interviewee determining their own answers. This is a key distinction from questionnaires where normally the researcher not only asks the questions but provides the answers in some sort of choice format, for example, ranking preferences in order, circling one item on a 'very satisfactory' to 'very unsatisfactory' scale, and so on.

2 The relationship between interviewer and interviewee is responsive or interactive, allowing for a degree of 'adjustment': clarification,

exploration, for example: *Tell me more about that,* or *I don't think I quite understand.*

3   There is structure and purpose on the part of the interviewer even when the context, like informal questioning in real-life settings, is 'natural' or at least naturalistic in the sense of taking advantage of opportunities that arise.

The criteria are most exactly and satisfactorily met in the 'classic' semi-structured interview; but this kind of interview, rich in detail, is not always possible, or necessary.

Context, resources and research purpose

Real-life research, which is likely to give the truer picture of how things actually are, does not take place in a setting designed for research. Conversely, a setting designed for research as in a 'laboratory'-controlled experiment may facilitate tidier procedures but produce results which are, to a greater or lesser extent, an artefact of that artificial setting, and lead to theories founded on too restricted a data-base. There is an unresolved tension here with arguments on both sides.

The 'real-world' researcher is constantly having to adapt or compromise on methods because of the constraints encountered. On the one hand, you can argue that this is the price to be paid for approximating validity; on the other, that flawed data-collection techniques skew the results in indeterminate directions. Many of the constraints are severely practical. People are busy, so they have limited time available. In an institution like a school or hospital it may be difficult to find a (quiet) place to carry out interviews; there may be political or legal or ethical constraints on what one can ask; people may be suspicious or uncomfortable about being questioned. And, of course, they may be inaccessible at a face-to-face level because where they live or work is geo-graphically distant – even on the other side of the world. Hence the coverage in this book of 'distance' interviewing techniques, which have their own limitations. But if you need to know what that particular person has to say, then you have to ask yourself: what method would be possible in this case? Better to have key data of limited amount and quality than none at all.

The different methods to be described form a set of options that will meet most conceivable situations. Each has its particular merits (and demerits) and these are summarized at the end of each chapter.

One determinant of which methods are used is the 'cost' involved in resource terms; and the main resource in small to medium-scale research is the researcher him or herself. The time–cost implications are a major consideration. It is easy to construct unrealistic expectations of what you can hope to achieve (see Chapter 4).

One criterion which can be a cost saver is that of judging which of a *range* of methods would fit the purpose of the research. Are 30 face-to-face interviews each lasting an hour-and-a-half really necessary? It is possible to adopt a 'pick-and-mix' approach to interviewing, reserving the more expensive methods for those interviews which are key and using other, less costly, methods elsewhere. This brings us back to the fundamentals of research: what are your aims? And what are the *research* questions you are setting out to answer in order to achieve those aims? A mind-clearing exercise here is to set out your research questions in spreadsheet format, and then ask: what method(s) would enable me to answer those questions? Good research questions almost point to appropriate methods. At the same time, trying to identify methods may suggest that some of your questions are not particularly well framed.

Inexperienced researchers sometimes rush ahead with their data-collecting methods without having specified their questions. Rock bottom for the present author was when he asked a postgraduate student what research he wanted to do: to receive the reply, 'I want to do a questionnaire.'

Distance versus face-to-face interviewing

The arguments for distance interviewing are almost entirely expedient: 'cost' is lower; access may not be possible any other way. It could be argued that the constraints on interaction are such that these techniques should not be regarded as 'interviewing' at all. Fitness for purpose has to be the main criterion for judging whether their use is appropriate, and this is largely a matter of common sense. Dealing with very personal topics via an e-mail interview will probably lead to caution on the part of the respondent, and a lack of cues about sensitive elements for the interviewer to be aware of. 'Distant' or 'anonymous' modes of disclosure are sometimes justified on the grounds that they will lead to less embarrassment and greater openness. What little evidence there is on this point is contrary. Nash and West (1985) carried out a study which asked adult women about their experiences of sexual abuse as children. All the women in the sample were first given a detailed questionnaire; a sub-sample were then interviewed face-to-face. In the interviews several of the women reported incidents that they had not disclosed in their questionnaire answers.

Disclosing personal details to an impersonal medium can seem like letting part of yourself go, but in an interpersonal situation where trust is established that disclosure becomes possible. We have to qualify this: the 'impersonality' of a medium varies according to the degree of pre-existing rapport: thus, you could use e-mail *after* an interview as a form of follow-up.

The reliability and validity of interview data

Reliability and *validity* are positivist terms, widely used in measurement psychology, for example in the justification of intelligence tests. In that context a test is judged as reliable if it gives consistent results either on re-test, or by measurements of internal coherence (different parts of the test agreeing in the metric sense). Validity is mainly judged against external criteria: in the case of intelligence tests correlation with academic performance. Since intelligence is a hypothetical construct, the value of such tests is heavily dependent on this kind of demonstrated relationship.

As Gaskell and Bauer (2000) point out (in a chapter which is recommended reading as a whole) 'it is axiomatically acknowledged in psychometrics that the reliability of an instrument sets the upper limits of validity' but 'in interpretation, validity may be associated with low reliability . . . the reliability-validity dilemma'. They go on to say that low agreement (reliability) between different data analysts may indicate that the material being analysed/ categorized 'invites a number of different and legitimate understandings' (2000: 340–1).

So, unless the researcher takes a very surface approach to analysing the interview data (simple descriptive 'categories' or the occurrence of particular words or phrases, for example), they are inevitably making some kind of interpretive construction of what the interviewee says. That it is done with system, rigour and reflection, and with careful attention to representative selection from the interview transcript, specifying the evidence for the inferences, does not alter the fact that a *subjective* construction is being made. There is a strange reluctance among researchers to acknowledge this.

In an interview, the interviewee is 'constructing' themselves in what they say, of course, but so also is the interviewer. Inter-subjectivity is at the heart of all social relations, whether in a research context or anywhere else. Acknowledging this does not mean that we get lost, as researchers, in a welter of subjectivity, rather, that we have to consider the role of this dimension.

Disguising the personality of the researcher

The way in which scientific reports are written has come under increasing scrutiny since the 1980s. Social scientists using techniques loosely categorized under the heading of 'discourse analysis' have drawn attention to the way such reports are constructed according to a certain orthodoxy. In particular, they point to the 'logic' of organization, the elements excluded, and the kind of neutral, detached language employed; the result being that the researcher is presented as curiously anonymous, typically referred to in the third person (if at all). This is not an argument for 'personalizing' research, but a query as to whether such formal discourse actually represents a complete or even a true account of the research process. This issue is further discussed in Chapter 21 dealing with the writing-up of interview data.

In an interview carried out for research purposes, the interviewer *is* the research instrument, and this means developing skills in facilitating the disclosures of the interviewee – standardized in that sense. But it is still one human being interacting with another and using their resources of inter-personal sensitivity to do so: the human instrument is not a machine. At the same time, the research interviewer has to become skilled at the task and cap-able of a degree of self-detachment, including awareness of any preconceptions of the topic(s) being researched.

Self-construction of the interviewee

The interviewee does not have the same degree of detachment or share the purposes of the researcher. They are being asked to describe or explain them-selves according to the question or topic focus of the interview. The validity (accuracy) of their accounts at least in relation to feelings, beliefs, attitudes – and behaviour – is widely accepted; after all, people 'know themselves', don't they? It is for this reason that interviews are the main method in much social research.

But as Irwin Deutscher pointed out some years ago (1966) people com-monly express attitudes verbally (good or bad) which they do not display in their behaviour, notwithstanding that they are often compellingly convincing in the way they talk of themselves. And G.K. Chesterton wrote, in an essay entitled 'The Return of Don Quixote': 'People are never more mistaken about themselves than when they are speaking sincerely and from the heart.' This is more than Chesterton's love of paradox. People have a working understanding of themselves which forms part of their ability to relate one to another: it is constantly revised through the process of interaction and reflection. How accurate it is is another matter.

We shall argue here that the validity of an account of a research interview lies not so much in whether it gives a *true* picture of the person but whether it is a balanced account of the interview that took place. That is different from taking the interview 'portrait' at face value; and in any case interview data, however illuminating, are only one kind of data obtained by one method. Increasingly, as the limitations of single methods are appreciated, the use of multiple methods, different kinds of evidence, as in case studies (see Gillham 2000b: 91–4) is seen as a more adequate account. See also Brewer and Hunter (1989).

The unique power of interview data

The strength of interview data is that they are often compelling. For example, after reading the statistical summaries of a large-scale survey – an indigestible medium – one turns with relief to a small sample of interviews of individuals whose lives are otherwise reflected in the characterless quantitative data. Comprehensive and factual though the latter may be, it is interviews that illustrate what it is like to be elderly and living alone, or to be made redundant, or to have had a privileged education. Such accounts are more than illuminating; they appeal to us because of their human character. This is about 'real' people not just 'statistics'.

However, the significance we can take from these accounts may overbalance our judgement. Politicians and journalists know this: in such media-skilled hands a carefully evidenced, reasonably interpreted general picture that they oppose may be destroyed. But a researcher works from different purposes and has a responsibility to use data in an even-handed fashion, not to serve ideological or populist purposes. Of course; but such traps are sometimes hard to avoid, particularly when we are not alert to them, because they may be part of our own attitudinal make-up without our being fully aware of it.

'Hard' and 'soft' research

Perhaps these problems of interpretive bias arise because one is doing 'soft' or *qualitative* research – that is, research which may have no prior theoretical commitment and is concerned to get close in to what is happening in the social world? Would one not be relatively free of these concerns working from a theory-testing model which sought more objective, measurable data, employing what are usually known as *quantitative* methods? Part of the answer is that methods have to fit the research questions, and suit the kind of data that one is seeking to collect. Methods are merely the tools of research.

Is not the strength of quantitative/experimental research that it produces 'facts' that 'prove' (or disprove) theories? But 'facts' do not speak for themselves, however they are obtained. *All raw data require interpretation* – usually theoretical in character.

Let us take an example from my own field. Psychologists interested in mental testing have often looked for patterns of inter-correlation between different tests, or different parts of a comprehensive test (e.g. of 'intelligence'). What we find is that some tests or sub-tests correlate more highly with some of the other tests: a multiple inter-correlation. It is not difficult to see several patterns of inter-correlation, particularly when there is a large number of tests or sub-tests in the correlation matrix. For example, tests which appear to have a largely 'verbal' content, or a 'numerical', or a 'spatial' content, correlate more highly with each other than with tests of rather different content. Psychologists then go on to say (tentatively perhaps) that they have found (or identified) a verbal, spatial or numerical 'factor'.

But in an important sense they have done nothing of the sort. Mathematical data have no name or identity; these psychologists are *interpreting* the data: saying what they think it signifies. And this is no different from a qualitative researcher assigning different statements to an interpretive category where there is an ostensible justification for doing so. Both are seeking to make sense of their own data. And both are open to challenge. Robert Yin in his book on case study research methods (2002: 26) writes: 'the "softer" a research technique, the harder it is to do'. One might add 'the harder it is to do *well*'. *All* researchers have to consider the possibility of interpretive bias.

Recognizing our prejudices

'Prejudice' is one of those terms that has come to be a pejorative: always seen as a 'bad thing'. In the sense that it is a view or an attitude which is harmful to others and is resistant to contradictory evidence, then it clearly is. But prejudices are often trivial: I am prejudiced against yoghurt. I have never tasted it: I just don't like the idea.

'Prejudice' means a state of prior judgement; and we approach everything in terms of that, whether researchers or not. All potential new knowledge is apprehended (understood) in relation to an interpretive scheme of our existing knowledge. Initially we cannot avoid understanding the new in terms of the old.

As a researcher approaching our subject, interpreting new data, we need to be acutely aware of that. It is not simply a matter of trying to 'keep an open mind', although being alert to unexpected findings or meanings is part of it.

We need to ask questions:

- What do I expect to find?
- What would I prefer to find?
- What would I hope *not* to find?

One is not always fully aware of these pre-judgements; they may even be unconscious. It is easy to cheat, in the moral sense, while appearing to play the game. Often, in reading formally correct papers, one can come away with the distinct impression that the researcher found what he or she wanted to find or interpreted it in a preferred fashion.

2 The ethics of interviewing

People are responsive to the apparent interest of an interviewer: and therein lies the essence of their vulnerability. It is sometimes extraordinary exactly what an interviewee may disclose to someone they have not met before who is listening with sympathetic attention. Curiously the element of professional impersonality (in the sense of not being in a personal relationship) seems to facilitate rather than inhibit disclosure. It is a commonplace experience for medical general practitioners, even when the disclosure is apparently unrelated to the purpose of the consultation. I once had this experience when interviewing a middle-aged woman (as part of a survey of employment conditions) who, almost abruptly, began talking about a baby she had accidentally smothered some 25 years earlier.

Whether people regret these disclosures afterwards (and their feelings may be complicated), the interviewer has a responsibility to them. You have been given, in trust, something about that person. It will rarely be so dramatic as the episode of the woman whose baby had died. But an experienced interviewer who creates the conditions for, and facilitates disclosures has a responsibility to the interviewee for how the material is stored (if it is), analysed and used.

Formal ethical procedures are now commonplace in research communities such as universities, and in the range of 'helping' professions, but their principles are also linked to a range of legislation (in the UK, specifically, in the Data Protection Act). The research activities, as well as the everyday professional practice of those employed in medicine, nursing and social work – but particularly the first of these – are regulated in fine detail. This is to protect the rights of patients, of course, but also to protect the professionals themselves because issues of consent or professional responsibility, if neglected, can lead to expensive and damaging legal action.

This self-protective emphasis is neither wrong nor unnecessary – quite the contrary. But its preoccupations can obscure the central ethical concern for the well-being of the patient or research subject. There is a balance to be struck, and for most people doing 'social' research the formal concerns are not as serious as they are, for example, in the health services. 'Interviews' are rarely harmful to people's health; and almost never fatal.

But interviewees may regret disclosures so that there can be harm in that sense. A research interview is not a therapeutic one, so it is important not to adopt a style which encourages inappropriate disclosures; and, if they occur, you may need to know how to deal with them. In the instance cited above it was necessary to draw on clinical experience to respond appropriately: it could not be ignored.

To avoid being intrusive, it is usually necessary to maintain a certain 'distance' in a research interview – friendly but not 'confiding' in tone. There are certain elements which help to set that tone, for example identifying yourself as a researcher and explaining the *purpose* of the research.

Identifying yourself as a researcher

Identifying yourself as a researcher (or as someone, normally a participant in a group, like a teacher in a school, or a nurse in a hospital who is also carrying out research) is an ethical issue. Doing so is bound to change people's perceptions of you to some extent. It may make them more cautious; but also it can make them more helpful. In any case, there is some effect but, for reasons of honesty, you have to accept that as an unavoidable consequence.

Not to identify yourself in the research role when you are acting as a normal member of a group, is to engage in *covert* research. 'Investigative' journalists sometimes do this, occasionally with dramatic results. But is it ever justified in formal research?

The answer partly depends on the extent to which the group being infiltrated is harmed by the outcome; and whether such an approach uncovers issues so serious (and which might not be evidenced in any other way) that the issue of the morality of deception is minor in comparison.

In the former category, Patrick's (1973) account of Glasgow gangs didn't do the gangs any harm, although Patrick himself was taking a serious risk. Holdaway's (1983) study of a police force (he was a police officer himself) aroused debate and some resentment because of his covert role.

The ethically 'safest' stance is that of being *overt* about one's role and purposes as a researcher. But there are degrees of this: approaches from market researchers are rarely very precise about what company they represent or the purpose of the questions they are asking. There is an element of deception here.

Without any sinister motives it is possible to be equally vague as an academic researcher or, at least, not to ensure that those you are seeking to interview are entirely clear as to who you are and where you are from. Your identification should include:

- the name and address (and other contact details) of the institution/ department/agency you are working from;
- your own role there (postgraduate student/lecturer/research assistant).

These are best given *in writing* along with very brief details of the *purposes* of the research, what the respondent is being asked to do, and what will happen to the information they give you.

Identifying the purposes of the research and what is expected of those taking part

People need to know what they are letting themselves in for. Ethics apart, this can become a practical problem if they find they cannot accept the researcher's demands, or feel uncomfortable about them. This is the issue of *informed consent*. Any difficulties here can be avoided by the provision of a simple research information sheet and a *signed* consent form. These do not need to be elaborate or excessively formal in tone. And they can be helpful: people respond more seriously to things that are 'done properly'.

Consider the following sample consent form (concerned with research about inclusive design).

About this research

- We want to find out how design could make everyday products in the home easier to use for older people (65+) living alone.
- We are particularly interested in how technology could improve existing products.
- We are also interested in problems older people have with new technological products.
- We shall use the results to improve product design.

What we are asking you to do

- Provide basic information about yourself (e.g. age-range; any physical disabilities).
- Allow us to interview you at home and to tape-record the interview.
- Allow us to observe you using products in your home.
- Allow us to video you using products that cause you problems.
- Allow us to keep this information on an electronic database and analyse it for research purposes.
- Allow us to quote from your interview (anonymously, if you prefer) in reports on our study.

- Allow us to use excerpts from your video ONLY WITH YOUR SPECIAL PERMISSION.

If you have any queries, please telephone......................................on

....

If you agree, please sign here:

Name in capitals:........................... Signed:.............................

Date: ....

Storing and analysing personal research data

A corollary of agreeing to take part in research is that people are giving you personal information. For legal as well as ethical reasons they need to agree and understand how this information is stored and used. And this needs to be made explicit.

The key points are these:

- *Confidentiality*: Making clear that there are restrictions on who has access to this information and for what purposes.
- *Anonymity*: This may or may not be an issue. If the data are not intimate or otherwise sensitive in nature, people are often happy to be identified, usually by first name and surname initial (David P.) and type of occupation. In writing up, a real identity does add something of authenticity to a report.
- *Security*: Paper information to be kept in a locked filing cabinet; computer information access controlled by a secure password, avoiding modes of transmission which are easily intercepted: all of these precautions are more relevant if the data are highly personal or sensitive.
- *Publication*: Most people will understand that research is published or, if unpublished as in a thesis, is otherwise accessible. Whatever the kind of output, it should be specified to participants.
- *Summary publicity*: Research sometimes gets media attention; often enough distorted, sometimes flagrantly. This can be unavoidable but the impact is diluted if participants have been sent a balanced, brief and readable account of the study's findings.
- *Exceptional uses*: You may want to use video excerpts for presentation purposes: in the example given, of older people having problems with household products, to an audience of designers. *Explicit permission needs to be obtained for this.*

- *Data lifetime*: Many of us have come across mouldering data about individuals in filing cabinets: the residuum of long-dead research projects. Data destruction when they have served their purpose should be a routine (and explicit) form of protection.

The right of interviewees to review the transcript of their interview

Have we not all at some time regretted something we said? And wished we could go back and delete or change it? Our tongue can run away with us, even if we normally have a sophisticated internal censor at work. Politicians in the relaxed atmosphere of a private dinner party may drop their guard and say something that appears in newspaper headlines the next morning: perhaps with damaging effects on their career and credibility. There is little sympathy with such indiscretions from journalists, the public at large, or their own kind. That's politics.

It is rare that what is said in a research interview ever approaches such a sensational character. But interviews are a form of record and it may be that an interviewee is left with a feeling that they have been unfair, or inaccurate, or indiscreet. At a more basic level they might simply like to be reminded of what they said. At the 'consent' stage they can be asked if they would like to check a copy of the interview transcript. Usually they will not take up the offer but it is a matter of courtesy that they have been given the chance.

In some kind of interviews this review stage may be a form of confirmation for the *interviewer*: that the interviewee acknowledges ownership of what is written down. With 'élite' interviewees (who may, on occasion, be senior administrators or similar), this is particularly important and they will commonly make this checking process a condition of agreeing to be interviewed; and will want to be very clear how the content is to be used (see Chapter 8).

Gender, racial and social class issues

One dimension of ethical standards is that of sensitivity to differences between the interviewer and interviewee and the extent to which these may inhibit, offend or disadvantage the interviewee.

Differences of gender, race and perceived social class may not matter in a particular instance, but they are commonly seen as dimensions of power. Courtesy and respect will dilute the relevance of this variable, yet there is a wealth of evidence about the effect on disclosure, and personal comfort, in such cases.

It is partly a matter of topic. Few women are going to be comfortable being interviewed about breast cancer by a male interviewer. On more gender-neutral topics that may be unimportant; although it should be noted that in some cultural groups (Muslim women, for example) interviews by a male researcher would be unacceptable on any topic.

Race and perceived social class are complex issues: the potency of the latter is curiously persistent and powerful, leading to an intrusive sense of dis-ease in an interview situation. Differences in the use of the 'English' language and cultural background can present hidden barriers to communication and understanding; 'regional' differences may be equally as potent (in the UK, the 'smooth' southerner versus the rest).

There are no general rules apart from the need to be alert to these confounding factors, not least in the interpretation of what people tell you.

Issues surrounding vulnerable or dependent groups

The first issue that has to be considered is that of consent. In the case of children and, for example, adults with severe learning disabilities, in some cases very ill or elderly people, while their personal consent should be sought, formal consent from a guardian or relative is also required. There is a thin line, sometimes, between consent and exploitation, mild though the latter may be. Such consent by others does not detract from the integrity of the individual being interviewed. It simply adds to the protection of their interests, which they may not be capable of fully appreciating.

A different case is one where the respondents are in a professionally dependent relationship with the researchers. The dimension of power qualifies the freedom of consent. That widely used group of research subjects, the student population, are both readily available and easily identified or classified. But if their tutor asks them to complete a questionnaire or take part in an interview, it may be difficult for them to say 'no'. It is the researcher's responsibility to be aware of this, make the freedom of choice clear, and MEAN IT!

Ensuring the safety and well-being of research subjects

Safety is as much an ethical issue as a practical one. It applies particularly where the subjects of the research are invited on to the researcher's insti-tutional premises. Whatever 'formal' safety procedures are in place, translating these into specifics and what is appropriate to the individuals who are involved is the responsibility of the researcher.

Key issues are:

- Clear allocation of responsibility for the care of children and other vulnerable groups. Note that this is a distinct responsibility, not just one added into the researcher role – though everyone has to be alert to safety issues.

- A clear demarcation of responsibility between carers and researchers.
- Vetting the status of those professionally involved.
- Ensuring the safety of the situation or equipment.
- The identification of potential risks – particularly where they cannot be eliminated.
- Ensuring that legal requirements are met.
- Checking insurance cover.

Large institutions are required to have a safety officer who can advise in specific instances.

Protecting identity information

Such protection is more than just a matter of 'confidentiality'; it has become a formal, legal responsibility, in the UK, enshrined in the 1984 Data Protection Act, which is in turn qualified by directives from the European Union. Although the Act (designed to protect individuals' privacy) has been on the statute books for over 20 years, its implications have been slow to penetrate the detail of practice, and there are widely publicized misunderstandings.

The working of the Act is overseen by the Data Protection Registrar and the current state of the applicability of this complex piece of legislation can be checked from the DPR's 'Homepage' at http://www.open.gov.uk/dpr/dprhome.htm.

Until 2007 the Act only applies to data held electronically (because this is the least secure, usually, and the most open to abuse). From then on, data which are held 'manually' on paper systems only, will also be covered. Depending on the scale and character of the project, it may be necessary to *register* – normally through your institution where there should be someone specifically able to advise you.

Formal requirements apart, people appear to have become more sensitive about providing personal information. Questions about income or sexual orientation, for example, may be seen as intrusive or indeed, offensive. You need to be very clear that such information is actually necessary to your research and not likely to discourage cooperation. In the language of research these personal details are known as *subject descriptors*. They serve two main purposes:

- enabling the researcher to categorize individual respondents (teenage single mothers, from social classes IV/V, and so on);
- enabling the researcher to divide up the interview sample to see if

there are characteristic differences between groups (single mothers aged under 21 from those 21+).

This sort of factual information is best obtained *prior* to the interview as part of the information/consent process. It might include the following:

- gender;
- living with partner/living alone;
- in a stable relationship/married/divorced or separated/single;
- number of children;
- present or previous occupation (from which social class can be derived);
- age-range, e.g. under 20; 20–29; 30–39; 40–49, and so on – note that people are usually happier to indicate a *range* than their exact age;
- income-range, e.g. under £10,000, £10–£15,000, and so on.

But in respect of each item you need to ask yourself: *Do I need this? What am I going to do with it?* And finally: *Have I the right to ask it? How would I feel if I were asked for this information?*

Formal ethical guidelines and procedures

Research institutions like universities have ethical committees and procedures, partly generic and partly discipline-specific; mechanical engineering research, for example, is different from research into contemporary history, although both may involve human subjects. Ethical committees have the responsibility for reviewing and approving the ethical standards of research – at whatever level.

Research funding councils usually have their own guidelines, not just concerned with human subjects but also the standards and integrity of research. It is a requirement of those seeking funding from these bodies that institutions have an explicit ethical standards policy and procedures which are displayed on their website.

In addition professional bodies have their own guidelines and, in the 'helping' professions, these can be extremely elaborate. Studying these sources one can become aware of issues and dimensions that are not intuitively obvious.

3   The importance of question/ topic development

The most striking difference between an expert and a novice interviewer is the clarity, focus and *economy* of the questioning on the part of the former; and the redundancy and lack of clear focus in the questions posed by the latter. As with writing, this clarity is not easily or quickly achieved; behind any skilled performance is a great deal of specific preparation.

The development of the topics or areas of relevance to the researcher, and the precise wording and selection of questions, often receive scant attention in textbooks on interviewing. Yet they are critical for the construction of a research interview. Cost is one major consideration (it is a waste of time to ask redundant questions) but more important is whether the questions are really working to achieve the aims of the research.

The process of question development

In the order of things questions come first. Research questions (to be answered probably by a variety of methods) come, logically, before the methods themselves. But in reality it does not quite work like that: when you try to identify methods you may find you have to reframe questions (as Wittgenstein (1973) pointed out, it is a nonsense to ask questions that cannot be answered). As research gets under way, new questions emerge, even quite late in the proceedings.

To avoid confusion, let me reiterate that the broad research questions – to be addressed by the researcher – are different from the specific questions in a research interview: which is just one method in achieving the aims of the project.

For the purposes of an interview you may start by compiling a list of questions you might want to ask; you have to expect that these will be added to, or subtracted from, to yield the set of questions that will ultimately comprise your interview schedule. Writing down actual questions gets the ideas out of your head and on to paper so that you can think about them. It is also the beginning of the process of *organization*: constructing the interview so that the sequence and content of the questions make the best sense.

Identifying topics

It might seem that the logical order of things is first to identify the broad topics you want to ask questions about. But that rather abstract exercise is not usually adequate in itself (and is not the way most people's minds work). You will have some notion of the areas of interest but these will be sharpened up by devising specific questions.

After brainstorming your questions on to paper, putting down as many as occur to you, you can then review and reorganize them:

- putting questions together that are essentially the same (? redundancy);
- grouping them into the topics they seem to relate to;
- identifying the narrative sequence – how questions and topics lead one into the other.

It is this second element in the exercise which will make you aware of topics you had not initially formulated as such. And this may alert you, in turn, to the need to write further related questions; or delete some topics.

Other topic sources

Even if you are knowledgeable in the area of your research, there are limits to your ability to identify all important or relevant topics. Most of us have had the experience of coming across a key element in a book or paper we are reading, which had not occurred to us, or the experience of a colleague saying: '*What about . . .?*' This can happen fortuitously but it is better to seek it out in an active and systematic fashion by:

- carrying out a comprehensive literature review because research shouldn't take place in a vacuum: you need to know what's known – and pick up clues that *you* could pursue productively;
- asking for independent suggestions from those more-or-less knowledgeable in your research area.

Carrying out a literature review is a book topic in itself (see Hart 1998). Harnessing the ideas of other people can be done in various ways: corrections to your own draft interview schedules (through progressive trialling and feedback); by discussion; and, most independently, by a variant of the *Delphi technique*.

The Delphi technique is most often used as a means of generating *research* questions, namely, the questions that are being asked in the project as a whole and probably answered by a variety of methods. Framing research questions, like the wording of interview questions, is as much art as science: some people seem to have a flair for it and even if they don't, they might well think of angles that hadn't occurred to you.

The trouble with discussion or showing others your draft lists is that you 'contaminate' their possible original contribution. In the Delphi technique you identify the overall research topic but not the questions you have constructed. Usually you ask two or three people to write three research questions – without knowledge of what you have written so far – and then you compare the lists. Both agreement and disagreement (or supplement) are useful.

Similarly, you can ask others to carry out the personal brainstorming exercise of writing *interview* questions. And, again, agreement and supplement are useful. Questions that agree with some of your ideas suggest you're on the right lines; questions you hadn't thought of extend your range; by adding these to your lists you can proceed to the next stage of pruning and revising and sorting them into provisional topic categories and narrative sequence.

Pruning and revising possible questions

It is important not to be too hasty about this. 'Pruning' may not be the right metaphor: 'boiling down' might be more appropriate, reducing questions to their essentials. The first stage is to sort what you have. You do this in two steps:

1 grouping the questions into topic categories;
2 then setting out *different* questions in some kind of logical 'narrative' order, with more-or-less equivalent questions in parallel.

An example is given in the box. Here the whole interview is about how students are coping with the demands of doing a postgraduate research degree. The *topic* is that of personal finance. Five distinct questions are identified; two of them have variants obtained in various ways, as outlined above.

- How difficult is it for you to cope financially?
- How would you say financial difficulties have affected your studies?

- How do financial problems affect your ability to study?

- What part does paid employment play in your financial situation?
- What kind of financial help and support do you receive?
- How do you think your difficulties compare with other students?

- How necessary is it to earn money to support yourself?

The researcher has to ask: first, which questions are the more important, and which might be deleted; and, second, can the parallel questions be deleted or combined to achieve an improved version?

You can put the questions into a spreadsheet format using Microsoft Excel or a similar system although my experience is that it is often quicker and easier to do it manually on to photocopied A3 sheets using the matrix format as in Figure 19.2. Low-tech has its advantages.

Whatever revisions are made, you still need to preserve the original spreadsheets. This is partly because you may need to show, or justify, your question development but also because sometimes you find that the 'improvements' are a mistake, and you need to go back to the prior state. No problem if you are systematic about preserving and dating the stages of revision. Of course, all this is desk-work and the real test of interview questions is trying them out with potential interviewees.

Improving question wording and format

Questions in an interview are meant to be said: which sounds like stating the obvious. But it means asking yourself: how *sayable* is this question? Does it sound natural? This is not simply a matter of how to avoid stumbling over the words, it is also a check on what changes you find yourself introducing when you say the questions out loud. More than that, it is a check on the *clarity* of what has been written down: if it is heavy going to say, then it is likely to be hard work for the interviewee to understand.

Clarity is a lot to do with economy in the use of words: the shortest questions work best – sometimes just one word: *why?* Any question of more than a dozen words is almost certainly too long. The following are key guidelines:

- Weigh each word: could it be deleted? Adding words, especially adjectives, or subsidiary clauses – usually intended to refine meaning or make it more subtle – often just muffles the meaning.
- Avoid compound questions: one at a time has a more direct impact, making the interviewee focus on the question; so not, '*Why did you*

decide to take this course and how do you feel about it now?' There are two distinct questions here which require two distinct answers.

Trialling the questions

We need to make a clear distinction between *trialling* and *piloting*. Trialling is your first attempt to try out the questions you have developed via desk-work. But before the questions are ready for trialling, there is one further stage – if you are fortunate enough – and that is to show your improved list of questions to someone (a colleague or supervisor) who is experienced in this area and can make further suggestions on tweaking the wording.

Piloting is a try-out of a prototype of the real thing: a late stage where you have absorbed the lessons of development and have made detailed amendments. As with the prototype of a motor car, you have to see how it runs in 'real-life' conditions.

So trialling is the beginning of the 'live' interview: where you are asking questions of the *kind* of person who will be involved in your research study, but not a member of the group you will actually be using. The intended research group needs to experience the interview 'fresh' and in its final, developed form.

Note that this stage is carried out 'live' and face-to-face even if the interview format is not like that, as in distance interviewing. In developing a questionnaire (to be filled in anonymously by hundreds or even thousands of people in a survey), you still start the question development in this way. Whatever the end product, there is much to be learnt from a trialling interview with the kind of people who will be involved in the actual research. Initial trials need involve only a very few people: two or three is probably quite enough.

Conducting a trialling interview

You have a list of questions, under topic headings, which will be far longer than the ultimate interview schedule, perhaps 30 questions which have to be reduced to a dozen. You may not be able to get through them all in one session; not just because the questions are so many but because of the kind of help you are asking of the interviewee. You need to say: *'I've got far too many questions here but I want to see how they work, whether they're clear, which ones are unnecessary. So any comments you care to make, especially if you can't see what I'm after, will be a great help'* – or something like that.

But apart from what they tell you, you have to judge their response. Some questions, by the interviewee's response, clearly show themselves as *key* and productive: these are the ones you will almost certainly retain. Others will show themselves as clearly redundant; others will evidently need rethinking.

Make notes on these points against the questions on your list as you work through them.

This first brush with reality – actually using the questions – is often a chastening experience. There is no substitute for a practical try-out even with the most careful preparation.

But apart from the question-specific things, you learn there are more general lessons:

- what seems to make questions work – productive and stimulating (or the reverse);
- the 'feel' of the interviewing process, particularly important if you are inexperienced;
- a sense of those elements which give an interview its characteristic tone and set the direction.

Simple interview practice is one of the most valuable elements of question trialling. Indeed, learning *how* to interview, alongside progressive improvements, is a process of cyclical development with your thinking and practice in a continuous state of interaction.

Progressive trialling

The first trials of your list of questions will result in radical pruning:

- *Out* will go many of the questions as their redundancy or inadequacy is shown up.
- *Key* questions will emerge – those that really work.
- *Revisions* will be numerous – mainly of clarity and 'natural' speech.
- *Topic* groupings will become more apparent.
- *Order* of questions will emerge more clearly: one question should 'lead in' to the next.

Even after just a couple of trials, the shape and focus of the interview schedule will be clearer. What will also be evident is whether you are trying to cram too much into one interview.

Basically, you have two choices: to reduce the number of *topics* (areas of the research) or to reduce the number of *questions* under each topic heading. Or a combination of these. If your plans look over-ambitious at this early stage, then they will certainly prove so on the day. Pruning is necessary for these reasons:

- A well-focused interview works best: clearer, more stimulating for the interviewee, easier for the researcher to analyse.
- An hour-long interview where both parties are working hard is

demanding; much more than this leads to fatigue and a drop in data quality.
- Cost in resource terms is directly related to length (see the next chapter).

In many interview situations *you will only be able to cover a relatively small number of topics, each with relatively few questions.*

What emerges as you get nearer to the form of the interview you will finally use is that topics and questions vary in their *priority* for your research. You need to ask yourself: which are the ones I cannot do without? Which are the ones that are desirable but not essential? Which, at a push, could I dispense with? Even if you don't take action immediately, you can prioritize as a form of preparation for the pruning you will probably have to do.

Principles for selecting questions and topics

For some forms of interview, particularly unstructured ones, you can use only a small number of questions. You have to be content to pose the questions and see how the response runs – which may be by a discursive route. For different reasons a similar restriction applies to written-response forms of interview (writing answers is laborious).

Depending on how fine-grained your research focus is, you also have to decide on how many topics you want to cover. If you are circling round one main topic such as the financial consequences of divorce, your questions will be closer together. If your research focus is broader such as the experience of the divorce process as a whole, then you may ask the same number of questions but they will have to be spaced wider apart, each dealing with a distinct topic.

The latter broad-spread approach usually works better because interviewees respond better to questions that don't have the flavour of already having been asked. It also makes categorical analysis easier because there will be a clear distinction between the content of the responses to different questions.

The *depth* of your interview is also a factor. In a semi-structured interview you may not ask a large number of (main) questions; but you will follow up the interviewee's responses with *prompts* and *probes*. In effect, these are supplementary or subsidiary questions or modes of exploration which you only employ if necessary (hence *semi*-structured).

So, for example, in an *unstructured* interview you might ask: '*What's it like working here?*' – and let the answer go where it will. But in the case of the *semi-structured* interview you would have a list of prompts (reminders for yourself) which can be just simple words or phrases, for example:

- staff consultation

- relations with managers
- friendliness
- working environment

to ensure that each interviewee covers equivalent topics.

Probes, which are ways of getting the interviewee to tell you more about a particular issue they've raised, are more difficult to use (you have to judge when, and in what way to use them) and so relate to the more skilled aspects of interviewing (see Chapter 5).

In an unstructured interview you don't intervene in quite this fashion but you do what is necessary to keep it moving; in a *structured* interview the whole thing is pre-planned.

Piloting and pre-piloting

Once questions have been pruned and the order and structure of the interview re-organized, your schedule is very close to what you will be using in the actual research study. But all changes ('improvements') throw up new problems and these need to be eradicated where possible.

The 'pre-pilot' is a distinct stage from the piloting proper. You have something like the definitive form but you have not tried it out as such. As with trialling, you select two or three subjects, asking for comment and feedback, observing how they respond and how you yourself manage the interview schedule: further adjustments to points of detail will emerge.

The actual pilot (again with no more than two or three people) is where you use the schedule, *as you will in the main study,* not asking for feedback this time, but observing how it runs. At the practical level this will lead to minor changes. But you carry the process a stage further by recording the interview and transcribing it (where the particular method requires it) and carrying out an *analysis of content* (see Chapters 18, 19 and 20).

Preparation for using an interview is time-consuming: is all this trouble really necessary? The answer is: data quality is a function of the quality of the data collection techniques – and you can't do good research without them.

When, as part of the pilot stage, you *analyse* the content of the interviewees' responses to your questions, you will get a different perspective on the wording or emphasis or coverage of the questions asked: another source of adjustment. It is sometimes only through this detailed exercise that you come to see a particular question is building up problems for you at the stage of final analysis. And if you fail to deal with them now, there will be cause to regret it later.

The analysis of content is one of the major 'costs' of interviewing as the next chapter demonstrates; you need to be sure that you lighten the burden as far as possible.

4 Different techniques and the 'cost' development factor

This is a short chapter but it deals with issues basic to the feasibility of a research project involving interviews. In the world of material possessions the most expensive is not always the best, but it usually is. For those of us whose financial resources are limited, there are regular compromises in this respect: what is the best we can afford? And, to extend the metaphor: is the best necessary, bearing in mind our purpose? Or, as a variant, does the added cost add enough value to justify the expenditure?

To the lone researcher the main cost is in time and energy, for empirical research is a demanding business where it is easy to over-load oneself. One of the most predictable problems when supervising research students is to find that they plan to do more than they can possibly hope to achieve. Not that experience offers a complete insurance against this. Again the financial metaphor applies: even the more realistic of us usually find that the true costs of what we want are greater than we calculate, that there are cost factors which have been overlooked or underestimated. Point made: let us look at a hypothetical but exact example.

The time–cost factor

You plan to do 15 one-hour face-to-face interviews which will be *tape-recorded* – almost always necessary because this kind of interview requires close attention to the interviewee which precludes note-taking.

Preparing the interview schedule, as indicated in the previous chapter, is no small feat, even if it is a 'shared' cost across all interviews. If you do the job properly, you will be unlikely to need fewer than 60 hours of work for this stage: time well spent and a time-saver in terms both of giving the interview and analysing it. So we have *initial development costs*: 60 hours.

A one-hour interview with 15 people adds another 15 hours: but that is the least of it because travelling to and from an interview location could easily double that, so we add another 30 hours: 90 so far.

However, the cost-heavy stage starts with *transcription* (see Chapter 17); quite simply, people can say a great deal in an hour which you have subsequently to get on to paper. This can take between six and ten hours per interview; let us split the difference and assume an average of eight hours. That adds another 120 hours: 210 so far and we are nowhere near finished.

Analysis of the content is a difficult one to cost because there are several different stages, and progressive decisions have to be made, so it is not an entirely clear-cut procedure. It takes time to 'see' what's there. This stage can easily take as long as transcription; but let us take a lower estimate *if you are experienced*. Another 90 hours which brings us to 300.

And then there is writing up which requires a further level of analytic selection: deciding which quotations you are going to use, how in your write-up you are going to faithfully represent the balance and meaning of what your interviewees have said. Three hours per interview would not be too much: 345 hours in total.

That comes out at well over 20 hours work per interview for just one part – albeit a key part of the empirical data-collecting stage – in a project. There may be other data to collect, of a different kind; literature to read, digest and review; research aims and questions to clarify; theoretical perspectives to explicate; and so on. Reading through the above it can be seen that transcription is the heaviest single cost. For some techniques such as real-life participant observation and group interviewing, you make contemporaneous or subsequent notes. In others such as the e-mail interview (Chapter 15) and the questionnaire interview (Chapter 16), the respondent writes their answers. In highly structured interviews (Chapter 11) responses are so 'pre-organized' – as in questionnaires – that analysis is straightforward.

Some techniques involve a great deal of setting-up: group interviews, video interviews and telephone interviews, for different reasons, come into this category: see the relevant chapters (9, 12, 14).

Ethnographic 'interviewing' methods (Chapter 6), because they involve asking questions as and when the opportunity arises, are *very* expensive in direct 'contact' time: you cannot be continually bombarding people (at work or at leisure) with questions. Unstructured interviews (Chapters 7 and 8) by their very nature – your controlling hand has to be a light one – tend to run longer than the semi-structured variety. Once people get going on a topic that is important to them, you can have a 2–3-hour interview on your hands. In some cases, you may even have to return for a second session.

E-mail interviews and especially telephone interviews have to cope with a high resistance factor. These media are over-loaded with 'nuisance' communications and so have negative connotations which affect cooperation and data quality, and therefore increase the 'cost' to you in terms of the effort you have to put into organizing them – not least what you have to do to secure people's cooperation.

Making your choice

The whole emphasis of this book is on the range of *possible* interview methods, so that selecting them becomes a matter of choice according to (a) cost; and (b) fitness for the research purpose.

As a simple preliminary, consider these points:

1 Are all the potential respondents of equal importance to the research? If not, you could use less expensive methods with the less important group.

2 Even if all those involved are equally important, you can employ the high-cost methods with, say, half of the group and use methods that give less depth or detail with the rest. The data from the latter can then form a kind of supplement – confirmatory, cross-referencing, and so on. Remember you can ask essentially the same questions using different techniques, for example in an e-mail interview as against a face-to-face interview. Data *quality* will be less good but topic coverage will be essentially the same.

3 Using 'cheaper' techniques means a greater number of respondents can be included at the same cost: important if you want to extend the range or make it more 'representative' – see the discussion on survey techniques in Chapter 22.

4 You can start with cheaper, perhaps distance techniques with a larger number and then, selecting from that group according to whatever criteria seem appropriate, carry out depth interviews with a smaller number. This is a technique often used as a supplement to questionnaire surveys.

5 You can use cheaper techniques, treating your whole study as a first-stage pilot: it depends on the level you are aiming for. For example, if you are doing a taught Master's course which has a dissertation element, but aim to go on to a PhD, then less expensive (and more superficial) techniques could be used for the former, acknowledging their limitations and signalling how you would develop them for a more advanced programme of research.

6 Finally, let us turn the choice issue on its head. Implicit in the points made above is that the most expensive techniques are always the best (instead of *usually*). But it all comes down to purpose: the 'best' is what is adequate for the research task. And if that is one of the cheaper options, then it is nonsense to make your selection otherwise.

5 The core skills of interviewing

> [M]ost people don't listen, in the same way that they don't observe. Everyday 'conversation' is often a kind of jostling, with the nominal listener more or less impatiently waiting for his or her turn (and often not doing that – 'over-talking' and pushing the speaker to one side, metaphorically).
>
> (Gillham 2000c: 35)

There is a special kind of ignominy reserved for authors who quote from their own previous work; however, I can't improve on the above and it does make a key point. Careful listening is the central skill in interviewing; and it is not what people normally do.

Indeed, it is not what 'interviewers' do in many situations, especially on television and radio where they often don't allow space for a response, appear to be listening only so far as to score a point or, particularly with members of the public whom they appear to regard as inarticulate, provide the answer to their own questions ('*you must feel devastated by what has happened*').

The unimportant skills

Texts on interviewing still tend to be dogged by a 1970s' 'social skills' approach, though to a lesser degree as the mechanical, 'surface structure' notion of skilled social behaviour has become increasingly discredited. If you need to be given guidance on how close (or distant) you should be to/from another person or when to smile or use eye contact, you should probably not be in any professional social relationship. Social skill is not on the surface: it is in the attitude and sensitivity to the other person and this expresses itself in natural ways that the other recognizes as valid.

Is this anything more than 'being oneself'? Is there nothing more to it than that? The answer is that 'being oneself' in a performative sense is not easy. Cary Grant frequently said that for an actor to 'be himself' on the screen was one of the most difficult things to achieve (Morecambe and Stirling 2002). Becoming a skilled interviewer is a process of self-analytic practice, developing one's own potentialities and style.

Practising interviewing

This is different from trialling your questions or piloting the schedule, although there is much of value in seeing all these stages as part of interviewing practice, particularly the latter stage where you are simulating the real thing.

But all interviews have much in common, irrespective of content or indeed of purpose – in the same way that all kinds of writing have much in common. So skills, once developed, are transferable, and become part of one's repertoire.

If you are doing research as a student or practitioner, then you can usually persuade fellow students or colleagues to be interviewed and, from your own experience in the same context, you can construct a passable interview schedule, questions and prompts.

Questions	Prompts
1. How did you come to take this job in the first place?	• Career development? • Dissatisfaction with previous job? • Salary? • Job attractions?
2. How did you find it once you were in post?	• Different from expectations? • New opportunities? • Colleagues? • Management?
3. How do you feel about it now?	• Positive? • Negative? • Changes of view?
4. Where do you think the job is taking you?	• Internal promotion? • Moving on? • Changes in career plans?
5. What advice would you give to someone coming to work here?	• What have you learnt about it? • What should you bring with you?
6. Any other comments, points you think I've missed?	

Something as simple as this (differently composed for different contexts) will enable you to get a 'feel' for interviewing and also provide material for self-scrutiny. You need to become comfortable with the interviewing situation and the value of a schedule is that it frees you to concentrate on the person being interviewed. To be able to listen, you need to be liberated from other distractions: tape-recording the interview deals with one dimension. A simple structure for the interview, which you have assimilated, deals with another.

To repeat the essential point: *listening demands intense concentration.*

Seeing yourself being yourself

Once you have produced a suitable practice schedule, the next step is to video yourself using it. For most people, initially, that is a mildly traumatic experience. It isn't just that we don't speak or behave as we think we do; we also don't *look* as we think we do. Our normal view of our own appearance is from the front, stationary, and in the reverse image of a mirror, which at a physical level is not how other people see us – and to which must be added all the other determinants of how one is perceived.

Arriving five minutes early for a seminar with some postgraduate students I found one of them at the front of the class doing an impression of my lecturing style. Since I had missed part of the performance I got him to run through it again from the beginning. It was very funny; it was also an eye-opener. Was I really like that? Or anywhere near it?

Since the lecturing mannerisms clearly engaged the students, I left that dimension alone. But I videoed myself interviewing and used these tapes for training purposes, warts and all. At the same time, and almost unconsciously, it influenced my interviewing style; and from that developed a simple self-observation framework for students to use, devised as a questionnaire (see the box).

It takes a little while before you can see yourself with anything like detachment. But once you have accommodated to this novel perspective you can start to look more analytically and systematically, and decide where improvements are necessary.

Entry Phase

1. Do you give enough attention to 'settling in' the interviewee?
2. Do you explain the purpose of the interview?
3. Do you explain how you are going to organize the interview?
4. Do you give the *impression* of being organized and in control of yourself?

Substantive Phase

5. Do you 'frame' the questions, i.e. pause before asking them and then leave space for the interviewee to reflect on an answer?
6. Do you come across as patient and attentive?
7. If not, how do you manifest the opposite, negative qualities?
8. Do you rush in with supplementary questions or suggest answers?
9. Do you allow enough time before prompting the interviewee?
10. Do you show your interest in what the interviewee is saying?
11. How?
12. Do you miss cues for probing?
13. If so, where and of what kind?
14. Do you use a range of probes?
15. If not, which ones do you use/not use?
16. Do you give enough space before moving on from one *main* questions to the next?

Closure Phase

17. Do you signal that the interview is coming to an end?
18. If so, how?
19. Do you give the impression that you are appreciative that something has been accomplished?
20. Do you say so?
21. Do you check whether the interviewee has anything to add? Or any questions?
22. Once the interview purpose is over, do you give attention to 'social closure' – expressing your appreciation, the small but important courtesies one shows to a departing guest?

The above is not an exhaustive list but sufficient to enable you get to know yourself as an interviewer *almost* from the perspective of another person. Many of these lessons are absorbed without systematic analysis. Some require further attention to detail: we shall deal with these now.

The fine art of probing

Probing is about getting the respondent to tell you more about something where you sense there is more to be told. Sometimes this is done by asking another, focused question, but the most productive (and sensitive) probes are not questions at all, more like forms of responsive encouragement. The essential requirement is an alert focus on the person being interviewed. You need to have subsumed the purpose of the interview, the specific questions that make it up and, decentering from yourself, concentrate on the other person.

Probes are of particular importance in the more-or-less unstructured interview where you are not setting the direction with a series of topic-focused questions but allowing the interviewee to 'tell the story in their own words'. This is where your main skill is in keeping them going, doing no more than helping them expand or clarify or develop their account.

There are many different kinds of probes – more than are briefly outlined below – because they are the product of one's sense of how to deal with an issue that has arisen. It is a creative response, and one created in the moment. It is this which makes probing difficult: you can't anticipate *when* it will be needed, nor specify the precise kind of probe that should be used.

In probing, you are not 'operating' on someone – although the term could be taken to have those kind of connotations – rather, you are getting the respondent to do the work: after all, it is they who know, not you, and it also means that, in an important sense, they come to 'own' the interview, with your encouragement.

Clarification

People often think they are being clear when they are not (*they* know what they mean and assume they will be understood). But when they are asked for clarification, in part because we sense there is more to be told, the respondent is being required to do more work on what they are referring to. There may be more to it than even they fully realize. So 'clarification' leads to reflection, exploration and expansion.

How you ask for clarification is a personal matter: the words and phrases that are natural for you in your personal repertoire. An important point is that it does not have to be in the form of a question. Saying something simple like: '*I'm not sure I've quite got that*' puts the interviewee in the situation of having to help you – quite different from being interrogated.

Showing appreciation and understanding

Beware of bogus concern: the national epidemic of counselling appears to have legitimized a 'caring' approach which can be perceived as intrusive. I remember the mother of a Down's baby telling me of the social worker who came to see her and whose first words were: '*I know exactly how you feel.*' She didn't.

It is a matter of sensitivity and good taste to be low key in how you show emotional understanding, and you have to mean it. Something like: '*That must have been difficult'* – an observation as simple as that – will work better than crashing compassion. A question, with the right use of words, can convey the same quality: *'How did you cope?'* More subtle messages can release a response that might not be allowed any other way.

Justification

We are always making judgements, the foundations of which are unclear, and perhaps make little sense as they stand. An interviewee may say: *'I'm not good at dealing with that sort of thing'*, or: *'I knew it was something I couldn't ask him to do'*, or: *'As things were at work, I couldn't get any further'*. You may need to challenge such judgements about themselves or other people or their circumstances, making a comment like: *'Perhaps you're being a bit hard on yourself'* or asking a question: *'Why do you say that?'* In so doing, you are encouraging the interviewee to examine their own reasons: and to make more sense of it to themselves.

Giving an example

Sometimes just asking for an example can help the interviewee clarify their thoughts. People often use judgemental words like 'neurotic', 'aggressive', 'irrelevant': short-hand, rather abstract words, used in different ways so that you can't know what they mean and what they are thinking about. Of course, you don't ask for an abstract definition but simply: *'Can you give me an example of what you mean when you say that he's aggressive?'*

Relevance

Similarly, the relevance of a remark may need clarification. In speech people are often rather elliptical: they leap from one thing to the next. *They* know what the link is but it may not be obvious to the hearer (quite often it will be between people who share the same background, or know each other well).

But it may be the connection is something the interviewee needs to work out in more detail or otherwise reflect on. In any case, you say something like: *'I don't see how that follows'* or: *'Can you join that up for me?'*

Extending the narrative

Whether you are dealing with an unstructured narrative interview or a multi-topic interview where there are a number of options to distract the interviewee, they can sometimes cut a narrative short, or lose the thread or feel they've been talking too much and are boring you. In each case you need to encourage them to continue.

Part of the problem is that narratives are complex so that the route forward is not always clear to the speaker. So it is partly a matter of encouragement and partly a matter of picking out a theme or event which will carry the narrative forward such as: *'So what happened after your partner told you about the debts he'd run up?'*

Accuracy

Factual recall is a problem in itself even when the facts have a major significance. People are usually better with the *order* of things than about *when* they happened. And order may be important to an understanding of what they are telling you.

You can run over the sequence of events with them, for example: *'Let's see if I've got things in the right order: the first you knew about the possibility of losing your job was . . . and then . . .'* Doing that helps the interviewee to understand and account for things. At this stage the concern is to help people to express themselves as clearly as they can, not the actual 'accuracy' of what you are told.

Reflecting

This is perhaps where a *book* on interviewing is not really adequate. Demonstration and practice work better at this point, but practice combined with video self-observation provide an alternative.

A definition of reflecting is not difficult: it is offering back, essentially in the interviewee's own words, the key substance of what they have just said. However, the technique should only be attempted – and then in its simpler forms – once you feel confident about managing an interview.

What does reflecting do?

- It *builds* on what the interviewee is saying.
- It *focuses* them on an element which would benefit from further reflection.
- It *encourages* further exploration.
- It shows *awareness* on the part of the interviewer of the significance of what has been said.
- It *steers* the interviewee in a direction which is essentially *self-*determined.

- It can lead to the *discovery* of attitudes and opinions which have not been previously articulated.

To some extent, these are attributes of any sensitively developed interview but reflecting is both more subtle and less intrusive than any other technique.

Here is an example which, for the sake of compression uses reflection in every response; in practice, you would mingle it with other forms of probe:

- I can't say I actually made a *decision* to leave my husband . . . it just developed that way.
- *It was a decision that emerged . . .*
- That's right. It wasn't as if, well, one day I hadn't decided, and then the next day I had . . . I just woke up to what was happening.
- *You reached a point where you knew . . .*
- Yes . . . and there was no going back . . . I didn't feel the same any more.
- *So your feelings had changed . . .*
- Fundamentally . . . I couldn't feel or imagine what it had been like before. It was like I was a different person.
- *You'd changed fundamentally . . .*
- (Pause) Not that I liked myself . . . because I think he tried in his way . . . but it was no good . . . I couldn't go back.
- *Going back wasn't an option . . .*
- That's right and then it was that I knew I had to do something.

Note these points:

- No questions were asked.
- No judgements were implied.
- The reflected elements weren't a kind of mimicry (which can sound idiotic).
- The interviewer's contribution kept the conversation going on a level and in a direction determined by the interviewee.

Of course, in this fictional example – which is no more than illustrative – it is easy, and reasonable to say that such features have been constructed. The test is to try out reflecting for yourself and see what your personal judgement and experience show.

PART II
Face-to-face Methods

6 Ethnographic methods
The interviewer as participant-observer in real-life contexts

When we start a new job, or a course in a college or university, we have to find out for ourselves what things are really like there: the informal reality behind the brochures, prospectuses and job descriptions. We do that largely by observing: looking at what goes on, listening to what people say; we look at the work others produce; we read documents – minutes of meetings, notices on notice boards, working papers, and so on. And we ask questions of those we come into contact with. Nothing could be more natural, and one of the reasons for the appeal of *ethnographic* methods is that they seem the most naturalistic, the most 'real' approach to finding out what people do and think in a particular setting.

What exactly is *ethnography*? Very simply, it is the method of producing a written (and sometimes illustrated) account of a particular group or institution or local culture. The term overlaps with social and cultural anthropology but there is a curious convention that those terms are mainly applied to foreign 'primitive' societies about which we may know very little and where all aspects of culture and social relations are novel to the investigator. Ethnography is a term more often applied to sub-cultures in our own society: intravenous drug-users in an urban setting (Taylor 1993), the inner workings of a Roman Catholic comprehensive school (Burgess 1983) or Whyte's (1955) classic American study of street-corner society. The fact that the people in these 'local' sub-cultures may be every bit as foreign to a middle-class academic researcher as the inhabitants of a village in the Amazon rainforest does not seem to influence the usage.

The vogue for ethnography – as a method as well as the use of the term – is largely a phenomenon of the past 20 years and parallels the increasing emphasis on naturalistic, qualitative methods of research, particularly the case study (Gillham 2000b; Yin 2002). And, as in case study research, ethnography is concerned with the multiple forms of evidence available: getting people to answer questions is just one strand but it is what we are focusing on here.

Access

Gaining access to the setting is the first task for the ethnographic interviewer. It is a problem avoided if you are in the setting anyway, which is why research of this kind is often done by people whose normal work habitat it is. They (usually) have to make it clear that they are stepping out of role on occasions to be a 'researcher', but they don't have the problems of (a) being allowed in, and (b) establishing their credibility and acceptability once they have gained entry.

A distinction has to be made between public/private or open/closed settings, and, of course, the two co-exist. Institutions, for example, have a public face and a private face. A museum has a public dimension, self-evidently, and you can watch how people – staff and visitors – behave within it; you can ask questions; you can collect 'public' documents such as guides and brochures. But there will also be a 'closed' inner sphere where working practices, policy, and so on are determined. Access to the latter would have to be agreed (unless you worked there) which usually means the endorsement or sponsorship of someone in authority.

Sponsors and key informants

In almost any grouping there are formal or informal authority figures whose permission or support you will need: a head teacher, a police superintendent, a general manager, or as in Whyte's study a gang leader, known as 'Doc'.

Such figures are often 'key informants': they have a lot to tell you. However, their support is double-edged. In a setting where you are not otherwise known, the support of this kind of authority figure may mean that you will be treated with caution, even suspicion, as being some kind of 'spy'. It takes time to change that perception: you will have to prove yourself.

Identifying key informants also takes time: you must find those people who are particularly knowledgeable on the topics you are researching. They may not be immediately apparent or the most immediately welcoming. Indeed, you have to be a little cautious about those who put themselves forward because they may have a particular line they want to get across, and this may be one aimed at deflecting criticism (or what they think might amount to that). They may, in fact, actively seek to mislead you. So caution and a provisional judgement are needed here.

Cost and quality

What is already apparent is that this is a very time-expensive way of 'interviewing' people, especially if you are not an existing member of the group. It could be a matter of weeks before you can start asking questions anything like systematically. Balanced against this is the fact that this phase is analogous to the trialling of questions and the development of an interview schedule (as described in Chapter 3), an analogy that cannot be pushed too far.

At considerable expense you will only be able to ask a small number of questions of a limited number of people, and in the one setting. More than one setting multiplies your costs. So why take all this trouble? The simple answer is that the expenditure is justified if it yields data of distinctive quality.

'Interviews' carried out in this way give access to people who probably could not (or would not) be interviewed in a conventional manner. If you want what they have to tell you, you may have no choice. Having said that, you have to guard against assumptions that some groups are not 'sophisticated' enough to participate in a conventional interview. Linked to this is the fact that, if you have the opportunities – and the patience – people may answer your (latent) questions without your asking them, in the course of normal conversation; for example, in the ordinary chat and discussion of a staff-room or cafeteria.

But it is also in these settings where you can ask, naturalistically, questions following on from something they've said. You have to seize your opportunities when they arise; *and this means you have to be entirely clear what it is you want to find out* – and that is itself something that evolves over time.

Problems with naturalistic interviewing

Even if people know that you are a researcher, there are often limits to their willingness to answer questions in the context of everyday activity. They may feel that beyond a certain point questioning is inappropriate, leading to a build-up of resentment and irritation. At one point Whyte's sponsor, the gang leader, said: 'go easy on that "who", "what", "why", "when", "where" stuff' (1955: 303), referring to the researcher's understandable desire to explore the reasons given in response to a first question. It is easy to acquire a nuisance value so that you come to be seen as someone to be avoided.

But this places limits on the depth of the information you can get, a long way from the detailed exploration possible in the more formal framework of a semi-structured interview. Keeping it 'natural' is not easy, and keeping one's research enthusiasm in check is another.

Recording answers is a further and severely practical problem. In anything approaching ordinary conversation people do not audio-record or write down what is said: it would be a social gaffe that would paralyze the mobility of everyday social relations – on which you are depending. Visibly speaking into a dictaphone afterwards is almost worse; so one is reduced to writing, perhaps cryptic notes immediately after the 'interview', which may present its own peculiar problems. See, for example, Ditton (1977) who recorded his notes in the only private place (often on lavatory paper) when researching 'fiddling' and petty theft in a bakery. Inevitably such notes (and 'on the spot' notes in general) are going to be very abbreviated – little more than an aide-mémoire to later, fuller recall. It is essential to write up these notes *as soon as possible*, while retaining the original notes as part of the evidence process. If you don't do this, they very soon become less than completely comprehensible, so that data are lost.

Putting what you are told 'in context'

What you are told is not the whole story. That is true even when the interview data are more extended and more 'in depth'. There has to be a context which locates the interview material, both descriptively and theoretically. When your interview content is more restricted and just one dimension of a wider social phenomenon, then it may be only partly comprehensible without the background detail being painted in. The interviewer has to be something of an ethnographer in the round.

There is the immediate context of the question and answer: how it arose and in what precise setting – a building worker on a construction site, for example – 'How did you come to take this job?' and so on. But then there is the wider context: working on a 'new build' housing site; for this particular company; the state of the house-building industry. All these elements support the meaning of a particular answer to a particular question on a particular occasion.

Single context and generalization

Most 'close in' qualitative research comes up against the generalization problem. To take the case of the building worker above: how general is his experience? Even within the same building site or the same company?

Obviously, the more systematically you 'sample', the more likely you are to get an approximation to a representative picture. But sampling in qualitative research is rarely of the kind used in survey sampling; its relationship to the latter is usually of the illustrative kind (see Chapter 22). Its main task is to give a balanced picture of what informants have told you and of those within the setting being studied.

To use the language of survey sampling, one may seek informants who come from different 'strata' within the group – in terms of status, occupational category, or degree of experience, for example. But this is more to do with trawling for a *range* of information than trying to establish a representative sample. People placed differently within a given setting can provide different information, and can suggest different ways of understanding it.

This last phrase touches on the different kind of sampling – *theoretical sampling* – that is characteristic of qualitative research. The actual information and opinions of workers on one building site (the facts) may not be the same as those working elsewhere; but your *explanation* (theory) might apply to other work settings. In other words, you may generalize to *theory* rather than claiming that your actual evidence is representative of the building trade as a whole – *empirical* generalization.

Gaining access to the internal world of a group is likely to throw up interesting evidence, but this 'evidence' is interesting because it challenges conventional tacit or explicit assumptions. The value of first-hand original data is that it can enable you to see things differently. And it may be that you can get this interview plus context data in no other way than by immersing yourself in the activity of the group, becoming a *participant* doing the same things as the people whose normal work it is, with the researcher role as an additional feature.

Detachment and participation

There is a tension here and it is partly an ethical one. The more 'detached' you are, the more you are 'in role' as a researcher. That is, you are being *overt*. However, it is often difficult to maintain that degree of separation especially if you are full-time, or nearly so, in a particular setting. Anyone who has been an 'observer' in a primary school classroom will know that children will want to show you their work, ask for your help, or expect you to hear them read: that's what adults are for. The author, researching the context of a school for children with severe and profound learning difficulties, and with an all-female staff, found himself effectively appointed in charge of games, despite a lack of talent.

The 'researcher' role became obscured and, in the day-to-day, forgotten. That privileged level of access resulted in opportunities that would have been available in no other way. But the overlay of usefulness gave to the researcher role something of a concealed quality. If people give you that kind of access, it does entail a moral responsibility: of fairness, at the very least. The ultimate value of ethnographic interviewing is two-fold: (1) that it provides data which can be cross-validated with other evidence in the setting; and (2) that it gives access to people who cannot be interviewed in any other way.

Summary

Positives

- high validity: naturalistic, 'un-guarded';
- can be cross-referenced to other data (observed behaviour, documents);
- gives access to people who could not be interviewed in other ways.

Negatives

- expensive on time;
- difficult to record responses immediately;
- only a limited number of questions possible.

7 The unstructured interview

All interviews have a structure in the same way that all conversations have a structure, however loose it may be. At the very least they follow the rules of language use ('grammatical' or not), of some kind of rationale and of that selective, more-or-less chronological sequence usually known as *narrative*. The notion of the narrative interview (NI) is one of the main topics of this chapter.

What an unstructured interview does is give responsibility for determining the structure to the interviewee who has to 'lead the way' and 'tell the story'. In research terms, there are three main uses of the unstructured interview:

- as an initial technique where the researcher is casting around for those things that need to be investigated in a subsequent, more structured, stage of the research;
- where the person being interviewed might be inhibited or constrained by a more structured approach;
- where the interest is in some dimension of an individual's life experience, and where the significant themes can only be elicited by allowing the individual to give their account in their own way, without the fragmentation of structured questioning which may lose the thread of the narrative.

Implicit in these uses is that the researcher does not know what is there, and cannot determine what needs to be known, or found out. The primary skill is in eliciting the account: of people's experiences and what they feel and think about them. The diversity of subject-matter can be very great: for example, being a female engineering student; the transition from school to university; what it's like to work in a busy call centre.

These examples give some indication of what qualitative research is about – the understanding of someone else's world – and where the researcher is concerned with *discovery*. The tacit assumption of a structured investigation, of whatever kind, is that the researcher knows what needs to be found out at a level of specific detail. If such a structured approach is to be valid, there has to be careful preliminary work of an exploratory and more unstructured character.

The unstructured interview as an exploratory or preliminary technique

Interviewing is often a preliminary stage in the development of highly structured instruments like questionnaires. That level of structure has to be based on prior knowledge of the area being researched. A starting point is to read the relevant literature and consult with those who know more about the research area; but what brings the topic into focus is carrying out unstructured interviews with members of the group or category the research deals with.

An example from my own experience is relevant here. I was asked to plan a national questionnaire survey of work satisfaction among university technicians. Although I had worked alongside them for many years as an academic member of staff, and so had certain impressions of how they felt about their jobs, I knew nothing systematically or in any depth.

The first stage was to tape-record interviews with a quota sample within my own university. At this level I was getting on top of the specifics of procedure, one that could be used across a random sample of universities at the next stage. Members of the sample were told the purpose of the exercise and then simply asked what they thought about their job satisfaction (or the contrary). I had no further *pre-planned* questions: this being characteristic of an unstructured interview. Nor did I employ standardized 'prompts'. What I did was to probe where I felt they had more to say (as described in Chapter 5).

Having carried out half-a-dozen such interviews I analysed them for *substantive* statements: those that really made a point relating to work satisfaction. This may sound a little vague but, in fact, these items of substance usually stand out quite clearly; and if you employ an independent rater, briefed as to what to listen for, the level of agreement is high (and where there is disagreement you have grounds for reviewing your judgement). The technique used can be summarized as follows:

1 Run the tape right through, listening for key statements but keeping the wider context of the interview in mind.
2 With notebook and pen to hand, play the tape again, stopping when a key point comes up and writing it down.
3 Carry out a categorical content analysis (see Chapter 19) grouping together similar statements from different respondents.

Not surprisingly, I found there was considerable agreement on the most important elements and these were often expressed in similar words. Not only were key topics being identified but *forms of words* that could go into the final questionnaire (and which could have a resonance with the larger survey sample) were being identified. The interviewees were, in a sense, writing the questions for me.

There is no need to describe this project further except to say that colleagues in other universities used the same topic-survey procedure so that I had a substantial base for the ultimate (quite short) questionnaire. That it was acceptable and worked well owed a great deal to the stage of preliminary *unstructured* interviewing.

Unstructured interviews can last a very long time – several hours – although in the example above I kept them deliberately short because of the focused character of their purpose and my own limited time. However, a very small number of lengthy unstructured interviews may provide enough material to construct a semi-structured interview (characterized by focused topics, pre-formed *main* questions, prompts to ensure equivalent coverage, probes where necessary) to be used with a larger number of people, with reasonable confidence that the key areas are being covered.

Preliminary interviews can also be used impressionistically to get a 'feel' for an area where you will be using methods quite other than interviews: experiments or intervention techniques, for example.

The unstructured interview as open-ended inquiry

Even if they have agreed to be interviewed not all potential respondents are going to feel comfortable with a more-or-less structured interrogative approach. It may be that only a very loose structure will be acceptable – nothing pre-planned, no schedule of questions.

That is one dimension. The other is that a loosely structured trawl may yield unexpected material. This is characteristic of the initial, exploratory interview but it can also be used as a main method where the kind of people being interviewed and the unpredictable nature of the topic indicate that it is appropriate. *Structure* will come later, at the level of analysis when you can discern and abstract those elements which serve the purposes of the research.

The unstructured interview as narrative inquiry

Before plunging into the practicalities of narrative interviewing (NI) we need to consider what 'narrative' is and its place in human psychology. Polkinghorne (1988: 1) defines a narrative as 'the primary form by which human experience is made meaningful . . . a cognitive process that organizes human experiences into temporally meaningful episodes'.

The construction of 'stories', like the construction of categories, is so built into human cognition that it is difficult to determine where this tendency comes from: that is, are the origins in the great variety of story structures that children experience in the everyday of social and cultural activities; or is the tendency something they are born with? As with the development of grammatical competence, the answer is likely to be a mixture of the two.

Certainly in the area of artificial intelligence (A1), one of the most intractable problems is creating for a computer that kind of knowledge, characteristic of even the youngest child with developed representational abilities, which is usually described as 'narrative competence' (Blackburn 1994: 254–5).

The developmental psychologist, Jerome Bruner, gives the narrative structure of our experience a central role in the psychological construction of self:

> I believe that the ways of telling and the ways of conceptualising that go with narrative forms become so habitual that they finally become recipes for structuring experience itself, for laying down routes into memory, for not only guiding the life narrative up to the present but directing it into the future. I have argued that a life as led is inseparable from a life as told – or more bluntly, a life is not 'how it was' but how it is interpreted and reinterpreted, told and retold.
>
> (1987: 31)

This necessary tendency for human beings to select elements and construct a 'meaningful' pattern for their experiences is a major problem in appraising witness reports: in retrospective recall, and without any conscious desire to deceive, people tidy up what they have experienced so that it 'makes sense'. Similarly, it is easy to assume that the researcher/interviewer by being 'non-directive' and not engaging in a question-and-answer approach is getting the 'true story'. What they are getting, of course, is the story as constructed by the interviewee.

Narrative interviewing: conceptual origins and reality

Credit for originating the narrative interview as a technique is conventionally accorded to Schutze (1977) and cited in Jochelovitch and Bauer (2000: 60). Developed as a critical alternative to the presumed convention of the question-and-answer interview, they outline the prototypical formulation as follows:

> To elicit a less imposed and therefore more 'valid' rendering of the informant's perspective, the influence of the interviewer should

be minimal, and the setting should be arranged to achieve this minimizing of the interviewer's influence. The rules of engagement of the NI restrict the interviewer. The NI goes further than any other interview method in avoiding pre-structuring the interview. It is the most notable attempt to go beyond the question-answer type of interview. It uses a specific type of everyday communication, namely story-telling and listening, to reach this objective.

(2000: 61)

To some extent it is a straw man that is implicitly attacked here. Skilled interviewing, of whatever kind, is characterized by the limited use of questions and a sensitivity to what the interviewee may have to tell us. And the assumption that an interviewee will tell their story without gentle direction *en route* is unrealistic. This kind of supportive direction is concerned not so much with *where* the respondent is going as maintaining momentum, helping them to complete or extend their narrative. Jochelovitch and Bauer themselves comment that: 'In practice, the NI often requires a compromise between narrative and questioning' (2000: 67).

The expectation that people will give their account in detail without 'interruption' is itself naïve, presuming, as it does, that respondents are readily organized and do not require direction or encouragement. And speakers who are getting no verbal feedback may start to doubt themselves, that what they are saying is not relevant or that, quite simply, they are boring you.

Structuring the unstructured interview

It is not difficult to see the virtues of allowing those being interviewed to give their accounts in their own way. But if you have an interview which is largely unstructured, at least by the interviewer, might this not mean that you end up with a set of unanalysable transcripts?

The answer lies in the prior identification of the members of the group to be interviewed. Do they have characteristics in common that will reveal generalities which, while they may not reveal a representative picture in the empirical sense, might lead to useful contributions to theory? This is the notion of theoretical sampling already referred to.

For example, if you are interested in researching the effects on people of being made redundant, there is a need to consider how the group is composed. The relevant literature, and one's own common sense, would indicate that being made redundant at the age of 55 is a very different matter from being made redundant at 25. If so, you focus the group accordingly; and this structured character of the group does not impinge on the unstructured character of the interview content itself: the 'structure' is external. Within a defined group you can still ensure the inclusion of individuals whose stories will provide different *perceptions* – different voices – bearing on the same context or experience. How one does this depends on the research questions: for example, is the experience of redundancy different for men and women of the same age? Breadth or depth?: qualitative research is always subject to these competing demands, but the emphasis is always on the latter.

The kind of research topics outlined above are 'episodes' in people's lives – the short stories of experience. But these can be located more meaningfully in a total life history approach. Our lives are a story with a beginning and an end even if the middle stages are somewhat untidy; and such an account may suggest forms of explanation that an episode might not, because it provides a context for discerning the operation of long-term factors.

How many interviews?

Deciding on how many interviews to conduct depends on whether the technique is being used as a preliminary, exploratory stage, or to develop a framework of explanation (*theoretical sampling*). Empirical data, from the first instance onwards, suggest explanations. As you interview more people, your provisional explanations are increasingly supported, qualified or expanded. Eventually a point is reached where additional explanations are few and relatively minor: so-called 'theoretical saturation'. You may decide to stop as soon as that becomes evident. The actual decision is likely to be enforced by the practical issue of time/cost. The kind of unstructured interview where you are actively supporting the respondent to keep going can easily run into hours (two to three not being unusual); you may even have to have more than one interview. We have already spelt out the total cost implications of this.

Preparing the interviewees

Although the actual interview is unstructured, there is much prior work to be done, because during the interview itself the researcher is not working to a pre-determined schedule where the respondent is being steered in a particular direction.

So assuming that the focus of the unstructured interview – the parameters of the narrative – is going to be an *episode* in someone's life, apart from identifying the group of interviewees, it is also important to ensure that *they* are clear as to the area or topic you will be asking them to tell you about.

They need to know this in advance, first so that they can decide whether they *agree* to the topic – which may be a highly personal one: the ethical dimension. Second, so that they can reflect on what they might say and prepare themselves: thus making the interviewer's task easier. You need to ensure this by providing a consent form and an information sheet (see p. 12).

Here the definition of the topic *as a narrative* needs to be carefully considered. For example, if women were going to be interviewed about their experience of breast cancer treatment, they could be provided with a specification to guide them as part of the consent process:

- We are researching women's experiences of the breast cancer treatment process.
- We hope to learn from individual experiences something about the wider picture.
- We should like to interview you, tape-recording the interview, so that we can get a full account.
- We shall transcribe the interview and then let you read it in case you want to make any alterations.
- We shall be analysing the interviews of a number of women and would want to quote directly from the interviews (anonymously of course) in the publication of our findings which may be in a book or papers in medical research journals.
- All transcripts will be kept in a secure fashion and will be destroyed within three years of the research being published.

The ethical dimension apart, this would mean that both the researcher and the respondent were prepared for the focus of the interview.

An interviewee's clear understanding of what they are being asked to do, and how what they say will be treated, are fundamental to setting the *tone* of the interview. If you demonstrate not just that you are clear as to topic but also as to the treatment of the disclosures, then that will affect the confidence and candour of the respondent.

Running the interview

A tape-recorded interview of some length means that you have to ensure:

- a comfortable interviewing room where you will not be interrupted;
- relative freedom from background noise (tape-recorders lack the selective attention of the human ear);
- a simple-to-operate tape-recorder with single-touch recording (the Sony TCM a39 is recommended);
- an omnidirectional table-top microphone (again the Sony ECM f8 is recommended);
- good quality audio-tapes (cheap ones can break);

- spare batteries and tapes for the recorder (the use of which you should be entirely familiar with) and spare batteries for the microphone (easily forgotten).

There is a tendency in any new development (as in NI) for a rigid orthodoxy to develop. Thus Jochelovitch and Bauer state: 'When the narration starts, it must not be interrupted until . . . the interviewee pauses and signals the end of the story' (2000: 63). One could cite similar orthodoxies from this interesting chapter. Here, we propose to take a more flexible approach – but the indebtedness is acknowledged.

Before you start: Even if you have provided the interviewee with clear preliminary information, the essence of this needs to be repeated, in particular emphasizing the significance of *individual* experiences for the more general picture. Being clear about purpose in this way means that the respondent is less likely to engage in assumptions of what the researcher wants to hear. This 'subject-construction' has unbalanced many a psychological experiment – often mysterious to the subject but nonetheless interpreted by them as to what is required. The interviewer should emphasize that exact accuracy of details is not the concern, rather the way the episode was experienced as it happened, and how they felt about it.

The main narration: Unobtrusively keeping this going is the main technique, in particular using the kind of probes that display interest and attention without interrupting the flow. But the ability of people to 'flow' their narrative varies enormously and some will require much more support than others, in a way which does not determine the content. It is here that *reflecting* is of particular importance.

Closing phase: In conventional NI it is at this point that questioning occurs. The form of these questions varies according to purpose and preferred style. One approach is to ask the respondent for their judgement of this phase in their life; something on the lines of: '*What do you think you've learnt from this?*' or '*On the basis of your experience, what advice would you give to someone else going through this now?*'

However achieved, the interviewee's concluding comments (often spontaneous) can be uniquely revealing. After the tape-recorder has been switched off and the 'main task' accomplished, people often find they have things to say that did not surface in the narrative. There are various reasons for this but one of them is probably the limits of narrative structure itself, that somehow it couldn't be fitted in, but is still felt to be important. Another is that the very activity of giving a full account often leads to a process of discovery, the articulation of which emerges in the more relaxed atmosphere *after* the interview. These additional comments need to be recorded as written notes immediately and retained as a distinct section of the data for analysis.

Summary

Positives

- useful as an exploratory technique;
- good for achieving a 'narrative';
- minimum 'interference' from the interviewer.

Negatives

- can be difficult to keep going;
- conversely, can be very long.

8 The élite interview

The term 'élite' can make people feel uncomfortable, carrying with it overtones of moral, social, intellectual or political superiority which are all the more unacceptable if they are true. But the term 'élite interviewing' provides a useful short-hand for a kind of interviewing which has a distinctive value. In short, it involves talking to people who are especially knowledgeable about a particular area of research or about the context within which you are researching. They are commonly in positions of authority or power by virtue of their experience and understanding. Relatedly they are also part of a network – of other people and institutions – and may control (or facilitate) access to these.

Such people are likely to be sophisticated subjects for interviewing. Not only do they know more than the researcher about certain key dimensions of the area but will also be alert to the implications of questions, and of their answers to them. They are not naïve subjects so will not submit tamely to a series of prepared questions. It is in this respect that the interview has to be loosely structured at best. And in so far as the researcher has a pre-formed idea of what they want to find out, they may find such expectations turned on their head because of the interviewee's more authoritative grasp of the subject. The response: *'You're asking the wrong question'* is a typical index of this phenomenon.

Access and control

People in positions of authority can be uniquely helpful; in some cases the research project would be impossible or severely constrained without their support. But they need to feel that the project is interesting and worthwhile; it will be seen as such particularly if it can be (and is presented as) of some use to them. They will also be aware that it may cause them problems. If the latter possibility is not considered and explored beforehand, the researcher may have their project blocked. If these difficulties are recognized and raised with the person being interviewed, then they can often be dealt with. The problem for such people is not that a difficult or sensitive issue might exist but that the researcher is unaware of the possibility. The naïve researcher can unwittingly set in motion a series of events which have nuisance value, if nothing worse.

Authority figures are also aware of the problems that could follow from any statement they might make. Careers have been ruined by something as apparently simple as the construction of a sentence or an unfortunate choice of words. The very fluency of practised speakers can lead them into this sort of difficulty; and while unlikely to lead to the more dramatic consequences, it can quite easily result in a 'local' difficulty or embarrassment which they could do without.

The problem is pre-empted if the researcher offers:

- anonymity (although the identity of high-profile figures can often be inferred);
- a chance to review and alter/edit a transcript of a tape-recording of the interview;
- an agreement to destroy the original tape once it has been transcribed (the late President Nixon had cause to regret this omission);
- a chance to review the edited use of quotations and associated commentary in a 'published' report.

This may appear restrictive to the researcher although much of it conforms with recognized ethical guidelines. But in fact it usually makes the interviewee less cautious and more helpful, not least because it reflects the researcher's awareness of the 'élite' interviewee's position and responsibilities. It is better to offer to do what you're probably going to have to do anyway.

Another aspect of 'control' which, again, it is better for the researcher to anticipate is to arrange to report back to the informant. There is a strong element of simple courtesy in this: if someone has taken the trouble to help you, it might be that they would like to know how you are getting on. But it is also probable that, as you progress, you will have further questions to ask of them and correspondingly they may be able to offer further help.

We now need to consider examples of the most likely types of élite interviewees.

The specialist academic

When I first went to university I thought all knowledge was in books: after all, one 'read' for a degree. Apart from the philosophical point that knowledge is a characteristic of the human mind and any other locations are simply forms of reference, I was soon to learn that many of my tutors knew things they hadn't bothered to write down. And I was scandalized to hear them make derogatory or dismissive remarks about some of those eminent authorities whose books I had read.

One of the things I came to appreciate was the academic convention that if you wanted to find out about a topic of which you were ignorant, you sought out someone knowledgeable and asked them. More than forty years later I still do that; and some return the compliment.

This process has not been rendered obsolete by the computer-based literature searches that have greatly eased the burden of tracking down references. However, these are most useful when you have already done some preliminary reading. And the best guide to that starting point is the (well-informed) human mind. Literature searches are an art in themselves, in any case. Specialist university librarians who have developed a flair for tracking across different systems, and interrogating them accordingly can be very useful in this respect.

Having said that, relevant references are not just indexed by key words. A characteristic of sophisticated human intelligence is that it is discriminating and can see 'relevance' by unlikely associations: titles that don't yield this dimension or use words that are not 'standard'. So referring back to the academic specialist for continued guidance is probably necessary as one tracks through the jungle of information. Depending largely on how interested they are, these experts may be willing to comment on drafts or reports produced by the researcher; the value to them being that it can be one means of keeping abreast of their area.

The advanced practitioner

It was mentioned above that academics often haven't written up their advanced ideas or latest thinking. In part, this is because they are not ready to commit themselves on paper but are quite prepared to enter into a discussion on where their thinking about their research is taking them. What may seem like the recent published work of an academic is, in fact, representative of where they were three or four years ago: they have moved on since then and the paper trail has gone cold. In addition, their informal comments or accounts may well qualify the formal published accounts: there are different levels of discourse here (see Gilbert and Mulkay 1988).

But this refers to an academic context where publication is the norm. In innovative *practice* which can be accounted as research in the sense of creating 'new knowledge', it is not so easy to find out what is being discovered or created. This is true in many practitioner contexts like medicine and engineering where formal publication and scholarship are well-established corollaries but where there is still a level of actual practice not reflected in this way.

It is, however, particularly the case where the notion of research as a *practitioner* activity rather than conventional scholarship is comparatively recent, as in colleges of art and design. Practice-based and practice-integrated research comes from a tradition where the 'research' process is not systematically recorded. Many leading designers can't be bothered to 'write up' what they do or think: those designers who do see themselves as researchers have to put their more formal research *in the context* of this contemporary, innovative practice. Interviewing is one way to research these contexts. Something like an ethnographic approach in a defined work setting may be required because capturing the essence of this kind of creative context is a major challenge. It may well be that face-to-face interviews are impossible: 'distance' techniques such as telephone or e-mail interviewing may have to be employed but in an unstructured manner, by raising topics for the key informant to respond to.

In the case of those who think *visually* and in the process of *making* there is a special difficulty in responding to verbal questions. It is not that they are 'inarticulate' but that verbal articulation is not appropriate, in that there are aspects, kinds of thinking which are intrinsic to the medium employed. While one might make a verbal commentary on them, a direct translation from one medium to the other is not possible: there being no equivalent. If we think in visual/observable terms, an 'answer' to a question may be in demonstration ('*Here, I'll show you*' – rapidly sketching out a design, a fabric sample, a prototype product). Collating and validly representing this kind of interview is challenging; the guidelines given in Chapter 6 on the ethnographic interview are relevant.

The expert administrator

Administration at a senior level, whether running a hospital, a police force or a commercial enterprise, is a political business (with a small 'p') in the sense that it is a position concerned with policy, finance, public image, power and control. Unlike the other two categories who could both be described as *subject* specialists, a senior administrator's brief is wide-ranging. Inevitably they are going to be more 'politically' aware – hence the need for research sensitivity to the vulnerabilities of their position. When interviewed, they will sometimes pick their words carefully (and this signals that what they are referring to is a sensitive issue or topic) but given the checking control referred to above, they can be quite remarkably candid. In short, what they provide is a different *kind* of information. It may be of the contextual-background variety, like the subject specialists, but it may also form part of the substantive empirical focus: there are special cautions here as to how one should treat this evidence. In the language of political journalism, it may have a particular spin on it.

We have discussed earlier how an individual's account of themselves, their personal world, is constructed according to preferences and habits of mind – a process largely unconscious. The administrator is very much more self-aware of how a given 'reality' is constructed; for the researcher this means that interpretation requires reference to other data (sometimes known by the inaccurate metaphor of 'triangulation' – see p. 164), as well as an alertness to the purposes behind what the respondent is saying. It is impossible to give precise guidance except that the attitude should be (for the researcher) to ask themselves: 'Why are they saying this?'

It is not necessary for the interviewer to tamely submit and let the narrative roll over them. It is both necessary and acceptable to challenge the respondent, who will be well able to cope with this even it if results in another oblique response. Like the 'black hole' in astrophysics, what is there may not be observed directly, only the effects on other elements which signal that it must exist.

The approach is an important one to develop, otherwise one may be stalled by a set of well-rehearsed platitudes that obscure a real state of affairs. People who have been interviewed many times before develop stock responses, a particular line, where either they are not really thinking or they are taking an established safe position. With that caution in mind it is reasonable to appreciate that the administrator's position is a difficult one, and that a guileless researcher could compromise it. It is not reasonable to presume sinister motives. And because agreeing to be interviewed may have an element of 'managing' that does not mean an unhelpful attitude; the interviewer's task is to release fresh responses.

Asking for further help and advice, after the main topics of the interview have been covered, may be one of the most useful parts of the meeting. Specifically, the following points might be raised:

- other people it would be useful to speak to;
- other organizations or contexts one should at least be aware of;
- relevant documents and other sources, whether published or not;
- dimensions of the research topic which one might not be aware of;
- general guidance on how to proceed: rules or conventions to observe, personalities to take account of, and so on.

Entering the network

Each of the three main types of respondent outlined above inhabits a particular professional world, which may be extensive of its kind. The academic convention is comparatively simple: '*I think you would find it useful to talk to x*'. In such cases an introduction is often a great facilitator even if it is only of the kind: '*Professor y suggested I write to you . . .*'. But whatever their special role, your expert interviewee is part of a network, which you may enter with their sponsorship.

The successful pursuit of research is a great deal to do with admission to these pathways of communication, which will not appear on any publicly accessible computer data-base.

Reporting the interview in the research report

A literature review of published research is part of a research report, but not all existing knowledge, especially that relating to professional practice, is published in this conventional fashion.

Where 'élite' interviewees have provided detailed information about existing research or practice that is unpublished, the convention of simply reporting a 'literature review' becomes inadequate. The account of existing knowledge has to include direct quotation from those authoritative sources and the role these data have played in carrying the project further. It may be that what they provide goes beyond what is known as a *contextual review*, to form part of the substantive empirical focus of the research: that is a matter of judgement.

Summary

Positives

- a rich source of information in a single interview;
- can facilitate and give direction to the research;
- provides access to 'unpublished' information.

Negatives

- élite interviewees can be 'politically' acute and controlling;
- 'hidden agendas' may underpin what they say.

9 Group interviewing

The notion of 'focus groups' is one of the clichés of our time, a term used by many who are probably not precisely clear as to what they are or how they work in the interviewing sense. Focus groups can be one method of data collection for the main empirical study but, as with other kinds of group interviews, they may be more useful in the early, exploratory phase of a research programme.

They are usually focused in two ways: a tightly defined topic for discussion (the *content* focus) and a specifically defined group of individuals (the *group composition* focus). So, for example, if the topic is the provision of nursery education for children under three, you might have several small groups composed differently: parents with children aged two to three years; nursery nurses; nursery teachers; pre-school educationists. For each group the focus is the same but the groups are differently composed. One can vary the composition focus: in the case of the nursery provision topic, for example, having different groups of parents: those with partners, and those without; those in employment and those who are not, and so on.

On the other hand, group interviews as we choose to define them here, and to contrast and distinguish them from focus groups, have a much wider spread of both content and composition. The open, trawling nature of group interviews indicates their main use as an exploratory study. They are particularly useful for the researcher who is entering a setting where *they* are unknown and which is relatively unknown to them. Here a group interview sometimes provides an early indication of issues that run deep – conflicts, grievances and the like – which may not surface in the more controlled context of an individual interview. Which brings us to the distinctive elements and characteristics of a group interview, however constituted.

People in interaction

How people behave, how they feel and think is not just a function of something called their 'personality'. People do have certain more-or-less stable
characteristics: tendencies to be domineering, or paranoid, or supportive or
appreciative of others. But whether, or how, these qualities are manifested
depends on the context of the relationship; and the composition of a social
group. In the latter case one can see a different side of people, perhaps not
evident in the one-to-one. But even here we have to be aware that the person
we know is not the same person other people know, puzzling though this
'discrepancy' might be. The novelist Graham Greene made effective use of
this difference in our experience of others – most notably in his film script for
Carol Reed's *The Third Man*.

The implication is that group interviews can provide different kinds of
data from individual interviews and so constitute different parts of the *multi-
method* approach advocated elsewhere (see Chapter 22). In some research projects it can be sufficient, in the empirical sense, to report these complementary
data, and then seek to explain them, for the main challenge to theory is
accounting for the evidence you turn up.

The level of structure in different kinds of group interviews

Focus group interviews by their very nature are more structured than the more
wide-spread variety, but only in their preparatory dimensions. Both kinds are
essentially unstructured *internally*: the group is presented with a topic, usually
not posed as a question ('*I'm interested in what you think about nursery provision
for two-to-three year olds*'), and then the person who puts this topic into the
arena – often referred to as a 'moderator' or 'facilitator' – by various devices (see
below) keeps the topic going.

Inelegant though the metaphor may be, the process is rather like throwing
a bone to a group of dogs: there are those who seize it immediately, trying to
appropriate it; those who nip this forward specimen to distract him; those who
watch their chance and make a sudden foray; those who watch suspiciously
from the outside, appraising, and only eventually picking up the bone – and
finding something tasty – after the others have tired of it.

This brings us to the special problems of managing and recording the
process of any kind of group interview, which can be a dazing experience if one
is not prepared for it.

Managing and recording a group interview

Published accounts of the process appear to make light of these practicalities, which are related. We have emphasized earlier that it is no easy matter to manage an individual interview, requiring as it does intense concentration from moment to moment so that one cannot easily rely on memory to recall significant detail – hence the need for tape-recording. But it is a feasible task and one that most people find, with practice and preparation, that they can master. Simply *managing* a group interview – 'steering' the topic, ensuring that individuals get a fair hearing – is an exhausting business: one's grasp of what is going on often feels somewhat less than adequate. And that is just one dimension; *recording* what is going on is quite another.

Tape-recording is typically advocated in methods texts. With respect, one can wonder if such authors have actually tried it, although studies are reported which have apparently done so. Perhaps it is feasible where all participants speak up clearly, identify themselves and, speaking like actors in a radio play, don't over-talk. My experience is that most group interviews are nothing like this so that such tape-recording would be, to extend the metaphor, like recording a dog-fight and about as edifying.

However, one form of recording that is less difficult to understand and analyse is where video is employed (see Chapter 12). It is easier to *hear* what people are saying when you can *see* them because the non-verbal cues that we use in ordinary listening are present; and it is also much easier to identify people because you can see them talking. It is also the author's impression that people are slightly better behaved – in the sense of turn-taking – when they know they are being videoed.

Joint management

Most texts on group interviewing state or imply that the interviewer (variously described) operates alone with the group which is typically composed of six to eight people – at least in the case of focus groups. But managing (even in the loosest sense) a number of people *in discussion* is exponentially more difficult than dealing with just one person. A simple quantitative calculation of the possible permutations of interaction within the group tells you that and, if tape-recording is impractical (as it often is), then the researcher is faced with the joint challenge of watching and listening to the group, applying a (light) steering hand where necessary, *and* maintaining some kind of contemporaneous written record . . .

This is clearly almost an impossibility for one person to do effectively. It is much easier to involve two researchers: one in the 'chairing' capacity, perhaps making occasional, very brief notes of the most conspicuously significant events, the other mainly acting as recorder but occasionally contributing to the interviewing process, for example, where the 'facilitator' seems to have missed a participant's tentative contribution. (Rather like an auctioneer's assistant who notices a cautious bid missed by the person on the rostrum.) And after the session is over the two can compare notes as to what appeared to each as the substantive elements emerging in the group interview – a crude form of inter-rater reliability.

A 'double act' is also easier in another way in that the partnership frees the facilitator from the pressure of lone responsibility, and provides them with someone, also a researcher, who can help to interpret and evaluate what happened. It also deflects that peculiarity of group dynamics in that they can sometimes turn on the chairperson venting diffuse emotions on an inno- cent but available head. Which brings us to the distinctive emotional and social content of group interviews.

What happens in group interviews

Gaskell (2000: 47) sums it up rather well in a chapter that bears the clear markers of reflection on a good deal of practical experience:

1 A synergy emerges out of the social interaction: in other words, the group is more than the sum of its parts.
2 It is possible to observe the group process, the dynamics of attitude and opinion change and opinion leadership.
3 In a group there can be a level of emotional involvement which is seldom seen in one-to-one interviews.

Having interviewed *individuals,* seeing them in a group context can be a revela- tion. There is something about an individual interview which promotes a more 'rational' view of self and context; and the exclusion or suppression of feelings, perceptions and events that don't fit this picture. With hindsight one can sometimes see that there were indications of these in the one-to-one interview. But it is their overt appearance in a group discussion which provides the background to one's perception.

Uncovering social reality is no easy matter and, as a range of evidence is accumulated, some of it apparently contradictory, the challenge of explanation (theorizing) mounts.

At the simplest level a group interview can provide an early indication of elements in a setting that might be missed entirely, if one relied solely on such data sources as talking to individuals and reading available documents.

The group interview as an exploratory device

If you are in the entry phase of doing research in an unfamiliar setting (or, indeed, as a normal member of that group identifying yourself in the different role of 'researcher'), then it is quite usual to set up an 'open' meeting – to which anyone can come – to explain what the research is about. And to tentatively raise topics that, on the basis of your present state of knowledge, seem to be relevant. You explain yourself as simply as that and ask them what they think.

This kind of preliminary trawling is part of topic/question development (see Chapter 3) and, because it will not form part of the more rigorous data-collection phase, can usually be carried out quite satisfactorily by the lone researcher. People are being asked for their help and guidance, and you are willing to listen and learn. Taking some notes is part of that.

Size and composition of the group

By the way it is organized (anyone who wants to can come), this is something you cannot control, and probably should not. And because anyone can come if they wish, then no-one has been excluded. Starting off with a restricted group membership (as with focus groups) can convey the wrong message.

At that introductory group interview you can explain that you will (probably) be going on to take a more focused approach, and you can ask for views, opinions and *advice* on this. For example, if your probable topic of research is support for probationary teachers (that is, post-training but before final qualification in the UK), you could ask for advice on the composition of such groups, for example, probationary teachers themselves; those with less than five years experience; heads of departments; senior management. That further phase is then seen as a rational and consulted development.

The limitations of an unfocused group composition

Observing the behaviour of a group, however composed, is a fascinating business. The composition of the group, not surprisingly, has a major effect on the participation of individuals. And the main dimension of difference is in terms of formal and informal distinctions of status.

In an 'open invitation' group interview – in a school or a hospital, for example – several levels of formal status may be represented. And it is hardly surprising that those who are more senior have a major effect on the degree and kind of participation of those who are less senior. The former may well have little to say: they have come to see what is going on, may only intervene when they feel it is necessary. But, even if entirely silent, their very presence is potent. It is the author's experience that they can often be identified by a more relaxed posture in the way they sit: being visibly at ease in a setting is one manifestation of authority.

And those who do speak may be affected, however obliquely, by their presence. There are other dimensions of power – gender, for example – and this is one that must be taken into account in the composition of focus groups. Women are sometimes said to feel inhibited in a group where men are in the majority, but this may be due to the fact that men are more likely to have senior status than any gender 'imbalance'.

Setting up a focus group

To recap: a focus group is focused in two main ways:

- in the specific identification of the topics for discussion;
- in the, usually fairly tight, composition of the group so that members have a particular interest in or experience of the topic; and are more-or-less equivalent in other relevant aspects. (For example, recently graduated product designers at the entry phase to their career, where the topic might be their experience of preparation for the job market.)

The *number* of those involved is generally not less than six and not more than ten; certainly, a group of fewer than six doesn't seem to spark things off, having a rather 'thin' quality in terms of the range of topics that emerge and the ensuing debate. In simple quantitative terms the number of possible interactions is also reduced in a smaller group. Ten is possibly too many (but better than too few). In practice, if you invite eight to ten participants you can usually be sure of a minimum of six turning up.

It is conventional to sit participants in a circle (no 'head' of the group and everyone can see everyone else). However, this has a rather self-consciously constructed quality that can be inhibiting because seen as a form of 'game-playing' or even manipulative. It is probably better to seat people around a table – a familiar way of organizing a seminar group with no awkward shuffling to get people into position. It also allows for ease in note-taking (again, familiar in a seminar context) by the researcher(s) involved. And if you do decide to try tape-recording, the recorder can be put in the centre of the table.

The role of the facilitator

As with chairing any kind of meeting the facilitator's key function is to ensure an even spread of participation, to be alert to those who are hesitant about making a contribution, as well as managing those who seek to dominate the proceedings. In other words, their role is to watch and to listen carefully. And it is to this evident interest in what they have to say that participants respond. They will also respond to evidence that the facilitator (and co-participant) is interested in the contribution of *all* those present.

It is not simply a matter of inviting someone to contribute (which may give the impression of dragging people in for the sake of some principle of equity) but watching for the non-verbal evidence of a potential contribution: *'You look as if you don't agree with that'* – depending on what the cue is.

Any opening remarks from the facilitator need to be kept to a minimum, otherwise the impression is given that they are 'in charge' when what is desired is that participants see the discussion group as the arena for *their* views. Beyond a welcome there are two minimum components of this introduction:

- who people are and why they have been selected for the group;
- what is the subject for discussion.

As far as possible, this 'identity' information plus some indication of the area to be discussed (but not precise topics, which need to come 'fresh') should be dealt with beforehand.

If the researcher is working in one setting, participants will know each other although perhaps not in all relevant aspects, and will also have been forewarned by a preliminary open meeting of the purposes of the research. In this case, just a brief reminder is all that is necessary.

Keeping the group on the topic

Research is about getting answers to questions. All researchers have some idea as to what it is they will find; in this sense, results can be anticipated or 'pre-formed'. However, expectations are not always fully conscious; and the most important research findings are those which surprise them and, ideally, the research community at large.

The caution implicit in this preamble is that one should be thoughtful and 'open' as to whether or not a group discussion is going off the topic. The framing of questions, the selection of topics always carry some level of presupposition. So when the group discussion seems to be veering off course – and it *may* be – one needs to be cautious, saying for example: '*It wouldn't have occurred to me that this was relevant: perhaps you'd explain.*'

One also needs to be alert to those non-verbal signals that show the course of the discussion, apparently running smoothly, is something that one or more members don't understand or agree with. The Cambridge philosopher, G.E. Moore, of great clarity of mind and exposition, said of his most famous pupil, Wittgenstein: '*Yes, I knew he was good. In my lectures he was the only one who looked puzzled*'.[1] The hitherto silent member of the group who says something like: '*I think you've got the wrong end of the stick*' or '*I think that is too simplistic*' can teach the researcher something; and also send the discussion in a quite different direction.

The role of disagreement

Being 'confrontational' has come to be seen as a bad thing in social contexts: the very term has acquired a negative ring. In the sense of those who have a routinely attacking or aggressive style, that may be a fair judgement. And, on the other hand, there are those who seek to smooth things down, to make things 'work'. Or do they? Freud is famous for understanding the need to make explicit and acknowledged one's inner conflicts, and for identifying the damage they can do if they are *not* brought out into the open. This may apply to groups as much as to individuals.

However, the researcher's role is not a therapeutic one; the point of emphasis here is that important evidence is not always on the surface, waiting to be picked up. And if evidence is overlooked, perhaps because it is concealed or difficult to access, then any understanding of the relevant social setting is going to be correspondingly incomplete, and may represent an entirely erroneous construction.

What a group interview distinctively contributes

A group interview is a quick way into a 'sub-culture', its particular conventions, concerns, and language. Hence the emphasis on its use as an introductory research technique. It can also provide an early indication of the *range* of views, attitudes and experiences, particularly if the group is constructed to include a representative range of people. It can indicate *priority* concerns and areas of agreement and disagreement: in the way outlined above. Strong feelings are more often evidenced in a group setting and in general there is more risk-taking (or 'wild talk' depending on one's own stance).

Because a range of ideas, experiences and proposals are often thrown into the arena, there is a greater role for speculation. And in reacting to these, individual members are more likely to define themselves in their relation to such novelties. Thus, you can identify factions or sub-groups among those present.

Putting group findings together

We have touched on the problems of making a recording – whether acoustic or not – of what goes on in a group. The earlier discussion of probable group processes and movements indicates how difficult the identification, selection and interpretation of these substantive elements can be.

A validating device is to ask the group to help you. Summarizing can be a means of asking for the further help of whoever is being interviewed – whether as an individual or in a group. Here you could say something like: '*A lot's been thrown up in the discussion and I want to make sure I've got it somewhere near right. Let me run over the main headings and perhaps you'd tell me if I've missed anything important.*' You then summarize:

- the key issues;
- areas of agreement and disagreement;
- topics which require further clarification;
- indications of areas that require further investigation;
- advice to the researcher.

And what can also emerge as a consequence of this checking process is *entirely new material*. This is a common experience for psychotherapists where something of central importance comes out at the very end of a session, partly because views and understandings sometimes only coalesce at the final stage and partly because, having held back, the client decides that they are going to risk disclosure after all.

The limitations of group interviews

If how people behave in groups produces material not apparent elsewhere, it has to be recognized that this is sometimes so patchy or incomplete that it provides little more than an indication of the need for further investigation, using a different method.

And if people can express views and feelings in a group that they might not display otherwise, there is also the potential for harm. Quite simply, people may subsequently regret what they have said. *A key responsibility for the researcher is the need to be alert to the possibility that the movement of the group discussion is becoming too disclosure-oriented.* Participants might find themselves revealing aspects of their feelings or personal history which are inappropriate and, at the very least, embarrassing to themselves and others. A group interview is not a confessional.

Summary

Positives

- valuable as an initial, exploratory technique;
- may reveal dynamics through interaction, and issues not apparent in individual interviews;
- provides early indication of a range of views.

Negatives

- can be difficult to manage;
- particularly challenging to record;
- data can be patchy and incomplete.

Note

1   The author cannot trace the source of this quotation; but it is too good to omit.

10 The semi-structured interview

It could be argued that the semi-structured interview is the most important way of conducting a research interview because of its flexibility balanced by structure, and the quality of the data so obtained. The costs are high largely due to the amount of preparation involved and the level of analysis, interpretation and presentation of the interview material required. The stages are clear (see Part IV) but, essentially, there are no short-cuts.

What does 'semi-structured' mean? In this context it implies that:

- the same questions are asked of all those involved;
- the kind and form of questions go through a process of development to ensure their topic focus;
- to ensure equivalent coverage (with an eye to the subsequent comparative analysis) interviewees are prompted by supplementary questions if they haven't dealt spontaneously with one of the sub-areas of interest;
- approximately equivalent interview time is allowed in each case.

These are the elements of common structure. The less structured elements, in the sense of not being pre-determined and determining, are that:

- questions are *open* – that is the direction or character of the *answer* is open ('*What do you think of the availability of abortion?*'; '*What is your view on providing grants for university students?*');
- *probes* are used according to whether the interviewer judges there is more to be disclosed at a particular point in the interview.

The central role of preparation

The preparation phase can seem like some kind of barrier, a tedious preliminary that you want to be done with so you can get on with the 'real' business of interviewing. Yet the success or failure of a set of interviews is largely determined before any part of the core data-collection phase of interviewing even begins. Half the present chapter is devoted to this stage, partly as a matter of emphasis because inexperienced researchers tend to hurry past it.

Questionnaires are even more vulnerable to this cursory treatment because of the availability of the kind of word-processing software that can produce something that 'looks good' – even quite sophisticated – for a few hours' work. This is the appeal of superficial characteristics, whether the product be a lemon squeezer, a CD player, a mobile phone; or a research tool.

The devil is in the detail

There are many analogies that point to the importance of the detail of preparation if the outcome is to be what is desired. We don't have to look far to find a common-sense example in our day-to-day experience. The DIY decorator typically skimps the preparatory work with results that are predictable. By contrast, the professional decorator appears to spend an inordinate amount of time with 'nothing to show for it'. But then, with an almost immediate effect, the final coat goes on presenting the sought-after pristine impression. Preparation has paid off.

Failure is a waste of resources; it is also a demoralizing experience. A lack of adequate preparation means going into the main phase of the research blind and blundering around with disastrous results. Even the most preliminary stages should involve a plan.

Research is about discovery, for the individual researcher even if not for the discipline as a whole. It is not about demonstrating what you believe to be the case. All of us are a mass of presuppositions and the researcher has to be aware of this. Particularly in a familiar setting we tend to think we 'know' what there is to be found out, when what we have to learn to do is to observe this familiar territory as if it were a foreign country.

So the first stage in preparation is to develop a naïve eye. This is where the exploratory kinds of 'interviewing' come in useful, particularly *ethnographic* interviewing (as described in Chapter 6).

Semi-structured interviewing is not a preliminary method: it has a developed focus on which it operates with a degree of precision, which nonetheless produces openness in the level and range of responses from the interviewee. The *setting* of that focus – wide-angle or the obverse – is one of the main decisions the researcher has to make: a stage that comes before the topic and question development.

Developing an interview focus

One of the strengths of the semi-structured interview is that it facilitates a strong element of discovery, while its structured focus allows an analysis in terms of commonalities. A basic decision is how wide your topic is going to be which has implications for how distinct questions are from each other. This was touched on in Chapter 3 but we now need to go into more detail.

Let us assume that the topic of research is women's experiences of the divorce process. Obviously this has many dimensions; for example:

- precipitating events and the stage of awareness;
- attempts at the resolution of interpersonal difficulties;
- the role of formal and informal advice;
- financial consequences and considerations;
- childcare and custody issues;
- effects on physical and mental health;
- changes in perception of self and others.

Now all these elements are woven together and you may feel or decide that they would best be covered in an unstructured, 'narrative' kind of interview.

However, in the more structured format that is the subject of the present chapter it is still possible to preserve this narrative element in the developmental sequence of the questions, even if the framework is more categorical in character. That is neither right nor wrong: it is a matter of choice.

Having made that choice, the decision is then whether to have a schedule made up of questions that cover the whole range of issues; or part of it focusing in on one sub-topic – perhaps, in the example given, the *health consequences* of divorce.

In either case the main task is to develop questions that are relatively distinct from each other, that, as the interview progresses, tap into something different. If interviewees (at the question trialling or schedule piloting stage) feel they have 'already answered that question', then it has to be deleted or rewritten. Avoiding this overlapping redundancy is easier when the interview covers a wide range; when each new question presents a clearly distinct topic. This is motivating for the interviewee and productive for the researcher.

It follows from this that writing questions (each with a shift in focus) is more difficult when the focus of the interview as a whole is relatively narrow, as in the hypothetical example of the health consequences of divorce (see the box).

Questions	Prompts
• Would you say that your experience of divorce affected your health in any way?	• Physical?
	• Mental?
• How did these health effects tie in with what you were experiencing?	• When apparent?
	• Changes from usual health problems?
• Did you seek any kind of help?	• Professional?
	• Other?
	• Friends, colleagues?
• How did you cope with those health difficulties in yourself?	• Attempts at self-understanding?
	• Changes in regime?
	• Self-knowledge?
• Were you surprised by the symptoms you developed?	
• What facilitated the process of health recovery?	• Time?
	• Treatment?
	• Events?

Here it can be seen that the depth of information and insight is going to be greater than asking one main question, even with supplementary probing. The vogue for 'un-intrusive' narrative interviewing neglects the usefulness to the interviewee of the support of a series of questions. However, whether 'narrative' or 'categorical' in style, the fact that you are circling round a single topic will encourage greater reflection on the part of the respondent. *But* the person concerned may feel they have reached saturation point earlier than in a more comprehensive interview. More focused interviews can (and should) be shorter, perhaps no longer than 45 minutes (as opposed to up to twice that length for the wider-ranging variety). One also has to bear in mind that interviews that go deeper are likely to be more exhausting for both parties.

The pre-piloting stage

To reiterate: piloting is usually divided into two phases, the earlier (pre-pilot) where you ask for critical feedback from the respondent, as opposed to the pilot which is a trial run of the real thing. The pre-pilot stage requires careful planning: in the selection of those on whom you are 'experimenting' (they should be the same kind as the research group, but not the same people), briefing them as to the purpose of the exercise and asking them to make any comments they see fit; and ensuring that, apart from this, all aspects of the interview are as they are intended to be in the main study.

Even at this late stage you need to be alert to what you are looking for:

- changes in question wording (particularly stripping any redundant words);
- changes in question focus;
- changes in question order;
- question redundancy or replacement.

In a well-constructed interview schedule one question leads into another and is, in a sense, a form of preparation for it. To achieve this facilitating flow of narrative response, where one 'chapter' follows on from another, you may need to adjust the questions to ensure a 'tie-up' or 'lead in' from the previous one. Or you may want to insert another, linking question.

In the same way that you sense 'a chapter is missing' so you can come to see that a particular question is, in terms of response, covering the same ground. This usually means that you have been reluctant to prune a question which for some reason you rather like. For reasons of cost and effectiveness any question that does not do a distinctively useful job should be deleted.

The stage of final piloting

Pre-piloting will have disposed of most points of detail; the final pilot involves something different:

- looking at the interview schedule *as a whole*;
- getting a *feel* for the specific process of this schedule;
- identifying *prompts*;
- carrying out a trial *content analysis* of these pilot interviews – a process which acts back on the interview schedule itself.

But first we must leap ahead, overtaking the actual conduct of the semi-structured interview (which follows), in order to look at what the stage of *analysis* has to contribute to question adjustments arising from the piloting stage.

Lessons from the analysis of content

This important topic is covered in Chapter 19 and we shall not detail the various stages or perspectives at this point. The reason it is being introduced here out of 'logical' order is best explained by an example from my own experience.

Taking over the research methods teaching of a Master's programme I looked at the submissions of students who were completing what, typically, had involved them in a great deal of work. A student had produced two volumes: one the overview of her research project; the other made up of the detailed transcripts, running to some 80 pages, of interviews she had conducted. But in her overview *she had made no use of those data*. It was clear that, having engaged in the enormous labour of transcription, she had found herself unable to analyse it. Largely this was due to ignorance of possible techniques of analysis but partly it was because the content of her transcripts was of such a sprawling character that analysis would have been difficult for anyone.

In an *unstructured* interview a widespread character is to be expected, the structure being provided by a focused topic and by the respondent in that they organize their own account (Chapter 7). But the student evidently wasn't aiming for that. One could discern that she had had in mind some kind of semi-structured interview but her questions lacked the guiding focus that implies.

A *semi-structured* interview anticipates analysis, and facilitates the organization of that final stage. And the way in which you find out if it does this is by carrying out a small number of content analyses (categorical in character) of the pilot interviews. If you do three such interviews for transcription and then seek to categorize the substantive elements of the interviews (see pp. 127–9), you can then judge whether the questions are giving you the *kind* of answers, that is with the required focus, you were seeking. It is only the painstaking exercise of transcription and analysis that allows you to see this clearly, indicating whether anything was going adrift during the course of the interviews themselves.

What are the main lessons of the piloting stage?

The specifics of content and focus apart, a familiar lesson is to find that you have over-reached yourself (or are in danger of doing so). The first warning may be that the interviews are taking much longer than anticipated. But at that point the full impact is not felt. It is the task of *transcription* that brings it home. The explicit time/cost calculations are fully appreciated only then. So you may need to ask: which questions (or topics) could be deleted?

At this stage there is limited scope for tinkering with individual questions: that level of refinement will already have been accomplished. It is possible that you can thin them out so that they are more distinct from each other. But you may find you have to delete a whole topic section. The key consideration is that topics (areas of the interview) are treated in sufficient detail; and that there is time in the interview for the answers to individual questions to be properly explored. Drastic surgery may be necessary.

Ensuring that questions are equivalent for all respondents

From the analysis of responses to individual questions come indicators of how to increase the equivalence of the answers you get in terms of coverage, and these go into your interview schedule in the form of *prompts*. So if a particular issue is not spontaneously mentioned, you can simply say: *'What about x?'* For example, if you were interviewing product designers you might ask the supplementary questions as shown in the box:

Questions	Prompts
• Where do your ideas for the design of a new product come from?	• Previous work? • New technology? • Everyday observation? • Manufacturer's brief? • Exploring materials? • Aesthetic criteria?

When you come to the stage of the main research interviews some prompts (derived from your pilot analysis) will prove to be unnecessary in some cases, but no single person will cover all of these points spontaneously. Perhaps they're not relevant to them but at least you'll have found that out.

Having covered these important preliminaries, we return to the actual business of the interview.

The conduct of the interview

This can be thought of in five stages:

1 the *preparation* phase, which begins before the interview takes place;
2 the *initial contact* phase: primarily social in character;
3 the *orientation* phase where you are pointing the interviewee in the direction you want them to go;
4 the *substantive* phase, the central core of the interview, the main empirical focus for analysis;
5 the *closure* phase which is partly social (but not to be discounted because of that) and partly cognitive, including an important review element.

Preparation phase

This dates from the time when you begin recruiting your subjects. Quite apart from the ethics of informed consent, making sure that people know what your research is about and understand what is required of them helps in the conduct of your research. It is more efficient, and this efficiency extends to consulting the convenience of those you want to interview, ensuring:

- the suitability of time and place of the interview;
- that they have *precise* information on the location of the interview room – perhaps including a campus map as well as room number and floor level;
- that they have details of how to get in touch with *you* if something goes wrong or changes have to be made;
- that they have a clear idea of the probable length of the interview – and perhaps a reminder that you will want to record it.

Efficiency conveys other messages: that you take what you are doing (and them) seriously; that you have been thoughtful about their convenience. These are factors which will affect the attitude of the interviewee.

On the day of the interview, basic arrangements need to be checked over:

- Is all the recording equipment in place, including spare tapes and batteries?
- Are the room and the seating reasonably comfortable? A shabby room conveys its own message.
- Does the room look organized and prepared? Tape-recorder, micro-phone, clipboard, and so on, set out as you need them.
- Are there refreshments available – water, tea or coffee, biscuits? People often have to travel to get to the interview but, more than that, there is a basic message in such an offer.
- What does your appearance say? People are not necessarily going to feel more relaxed because you are scruffily dressed. This is not an argument for a 'formal' appearance, but have you taken some trouble?

It is worth observing at this point that the interviewee is not yet in the room; and yet such preliminaries (often neglected in textbooks on interviewing) substantially determine the tenor of the interview.

Initial contact: social and informational elements

The components of a welcome require some thought:

- Introductions: *'I'm Gill Evans'* – not *'I'm Dr Evans'* which is off-putting. Note that a similar response: *'David Munro'* does not constitute an invitation to use a first name (which is cued by them using *your* first name, or they may just say *'Please call me David'*). We live in an instant first name usage society, but not everyone likes it and it is especially offensive from a much younger person (visit any home for the elderly to see this in action).
- The smaller, but still important details: an offer of refreshment, a question about their journey (*'Did you have trouble finding the place?'*); the comfort of the room (*'Do you find it too warm in here?'*); the location of the lavatories.

Orientation: explaining the interview

Here you are mainly amplifying the information you have already provided, but necessary because you are steering the person into the interview and, in speech and face-to-face, you can provide much more detail than would be absorbed in written preliminary details. And, of course, they can ask questions.

The primary task at this point is *explanation*: not just of the purposes of the interview but of the research as a whole. You also need to explain in practical terms why you need to record the interview. And you can explain how you do the analysis; and touch on the issues of confidentiality, checking whether they would want to be anonymous, and so on – the issues covered in Chapter 2.

You can also explain your use of an interview schedule and how you work it (*'I've got a list of questions here that I ask everybody, and reminders to me so that I don't miss anything out'*).

And, last of all (even if you've checked it before), try out the recording quality of your tape-recorder: there is a particular kind of stress associated with trying to transcribe a less-than-distinct recorded interview (*'I'd better see if this is working properly. Let's talk for a couple of minutes and then I'll play it back'*).

See Chapter 5 to recap the conduct of the central substantive phase of an interview – in particular, the use of prompts and probes.

The closure phase

The importance of the *closure* phase differs according to how structured the interview is. In relatively unstructured interviews the need for a review and summary in the final stage is because participants may have 'lost sight' of what has been covered, and what has not. In a semi-structured interview where the respondent has been steered through the topics of interest to the researcher there may be gaps of a different kind – those elements which have, because of the degree of structure, been excluded.

So as part of the appreciation of what the interviewee has contributed, one can insert a further check (*'We seem to have covered a great deal of ground and you've been very patient. But do you think there's anything we've missed out?'*). And you can follow this up with a more general trawl: *'Do you have any other comments about what we've discussed, or about the research as a whole?'* It should be emphasized that these questions are not just social in character – displaying courtesy and a valuing of the respondent, important though they are – but often add valuable material. Sometimes a brief follow-up interview is justified – possibly on the telephone (see Chapter 14) – perhaps two or three days later, when things are still fresh in the interviewee's mind.

What remains? Most important is the offer of checking and feedback:

- Do they want to see a transcript of the interview to 'see what they've said'?
- A double-check: how do they want to be identified or do they want to be anonymous?
- You'll be sending them a summary of the research findings but would they like to see the full report? Rest assured that few will take you up on this!
- Do they have your contact details in case they need to get in touch?

So closure is not simply a matter of getting people politely off the premises. It has a job to do, and there is a 'social closure' value in its business-like elements: a 'winding down' function to departure.

Summary

Positives

- provides a balance between structure and openness;
- with the use of prompts, roughly equivalent coverage can be achieved;
- analysis is facilitated by the level of structure.

Negatives

- costly in time (interview plus transcription plus analysis plus writing up);
- question/topic development a lengthy phase;
- skill/practice required to achieve adequate performance.

11 Structured interviewing
The use of recording schedules

From the unstructured to the semi-structured, and now to the structured interview. These have been presented as distinct types for purposes of emphasis and clarity of focus. In fact, of course, they are simply stages on a graded scale, capable of infinite variation.

The definition of a recording schedule

In order to distinguish structured interviews from questionnaires, the term *recording schedule* is used here – as in Moser and Kalton's classic *Social Survey Research Methods* (1986). Recording schedules, usually administered face-to-face but also widely used in telephone surveys, are the primary tool in social survey research. Hence the hordes of market researchers one finds in the main shopping streets of our cities and towns scanning passers-by to see which ones might be compliant and seem likely to fit the quota survey criteria (women 45+, teenagers, and so on). Such interviews focusing on 'big market' issues like TV viewing, mobile phone use, holiday preferences, are very short and often conducted with feverish haste.

Since the employers of these street market-researchers are doubtless driven by tight cost-constraints we need to consider why they use this relatively expensive, even if abbreviated, method of getting people to complete what is essentially a questionnaire – that is, the kind of thing that requires a simple choice response to the sort of question usually described as *closed*.

If a recording schedule is in effect a *verbally* administered questionnaire, why might it be preferred? What are its advantages? Let us invert the argument and ask: what are the *dis*advantages of questionnaires? We can list these:

- Getting postal questionnaires returned – referred to as the *response rate* – is a major problem.

- The ones you *do* get back may not represent a balanced cross-section of the group you are researching.
- Some returned questionnaires will be incomplete or reflect a misunderstanding on the part of the respondent.
- It is impossible to know *how* the questionnaire was completed, that is, whether anyone else was involved or consulted.
- Questionnaires can be extremely slow to come in and will often require follow-up prompting letters, phone calls or e-mails.
- People tend to respond less well (if at all) to something that requires a written response (however minimal).

The advantages of recording schedules

These are largely the inverse of the disadvantages of questionnaires listed above. But surely, one might ask, even allowing for a moderate response rate, it is more time-consuming to do a hundred person-to-person recording schedules than an equivalent number of questionnaires?

A recording schedule will usually take no more than five to ten minutes to complete, if well organized and practised. It is quite feasible to do 30 in a day – more, if they are conducted by telephone. And of course, you can work to a quota which is representative across the group being researched. Your hundred completed responses will easily be achieved in a week – with the advantages of data quality indicated by the brief critique of questionnaires above. So, unless very large numbers are involved, *recording schedules are to be preferred to questionnaires*. Distance is not a problem because recording schedules are well suited to telephone interviewing.

Of course, if your resources run to that, you can expand the number of such interviews by using multiple interviewers, but then you run into problems of training and equivalence. When you have been researching the area yourself, developing and identifying the question topics and the precise wording and order of the questions, then you bring to an individual interview a level of competence which can be difficult to match.

Developing questions and topics

Essentially this is the same process as for all forms of interview and as described in Chapter 3. The main difference is that the questions, as in a questionnaire, are mainly *closed*. Which is to say the *answers* are 'closed' by being restricted to a choice format.

These questions are of three main types:

- *Subject descriptors*: information about the person you are interviewing which can be used to subdivide the group – age, occupation and so on.
- *Behavioural*: what people *do* – for example: *Which of the following newspapers do you read?*
- *Attitudes and opinions*: for example: *How do you rate the government's policy on asylum?* with a rating scale (high to low, or very satisfactory to very unsatisfactory) Or: *What do you consider the most important qualities in an employer?* – with a list of qualities to be ranked in choice format.

From these simple examples it can be seen that a distinctive aspect of developing a recording schedule is in the way the questions are framed (and the restricted answers) not their actual content.

The same topic content could be covered (say, in a semi-structured interview) by *open* questions. Indeed, these techniques can be used in parallel to complement each other. The limitation of a modest number of 'in-depth' interviews using open questions is that you don't get a representative picture, while the major limitation of structured interviews using closed questions is that you don't get unexpected answers – and you don't know what lies behind them.

Constructing and conducting a recording schedule interview

Here we are only talking about the face-to-face variety; their use via the telephone is dealt with in Chapter 14. All interviews require clear choices and priorities in the topics and questions that can be asked. The time constraints/economy, which is one of the merits of recording schedules, make these choices even more severe. In developing the schedule you will need to be sure it can be administered within a tightly specified time limit. It may be that people will only agree if they know it will take no more than, say, ten minutes. *And if you specify that, you must keep to it.*

So every question, of whatever kind, has to be really necessary. In the *subject descriptors* section, for example, are you sure that you need *all* the information you might ask? Common-sense criteria have to be applied: most people would understand that information on age and occupation might be necessary. But questions about income or educational level start to feel a bit intrusive, although it depends how they are asked.

The design of a recording schedule

A questionnaire which has to be filled in by the respondent (and usually sent through the post) requires careful design and development so that its use is clear to the person completing it (see the review of what is involved in Gillham 2000a: 15–44).

But in a recording schedule the written responses are recorded by the researcher; the respondent either has to answer a spoken question or indicate a choice from a card which gives a range of answers. So a recording schedule can be much more summary and 'bare bones': the main requirements being that it is quick and unambiguous for the interviewer to record the respondent's answer or choice.

The basic elements are:

- the question the interviewer has to ask;
- the prompt to produce the (numbered) show card;
- a simple way of recording the answer, e.g. circling a letter for the choice made.

The examples given below in discussing different types of question/choice formats make this clear. It can be seen that this kind of record not only makes for a quickly administered interview but also for one which is quick and simple to analyse.

The use of 'show cards'

It might seem paradoxical to have a face-to-face interview where people are given things to read (or look at) but there are good reasons for this. Here is an example of an age-range response show card:

Question: Please look at this card. From **a** to **g** which is your age-range?		
a under 20	**e** 50–59	
b 20–29	**f** 60–69	
c 30–39	**g** 70 and above	
d 40–49		

The advantages are:

- It would be tedious to read out the whole question including the age-ranges (and people might 'lose the place' and have to ask you to repeat it).

- People are usually more willing to give an age-*range* particularly if it is identified by a letter.
- At each level *wider* ranges are more acceptable and usually all that is necessary for purposes of analysis; this applies to income ranges as well.

What you are showing people has the advantage of being quicker but also has another advantage – that of simultaneity: the choice elements are all there at the same time. Let us take another example where respondents are being asked to select a response from a list (the newspaper they most often read):

Question: Please look at this card. Which daily newspaper do you read most often?

a   The *Sun*
b   The *Daily Mail*
c   *The Times*
d   The *Daily Express*
e   The *Daily Telegraph*
f   The *Independent*
g   *The Guardian*
h   The *Daily Mirror*
i   *The Financial Times*
j   Any other: please name

Show cards don't have to be textual. In market research, for example, you might be shown a set of logos and asked whether you recognize them; or your preference for prototype logos not yet in use. A range of answer formats is possible but they essentially boil down to recognition/choice/attitude/preference and selecting one or more answers.

Different kinds of answer formats

Although the number of basic formats is not large, it is possible to adapt or develop them. In the example given above you could ask, additionally, such questions as: *Is there any other paper that you read almost as often?* or: *Is there any paper that you never read?* and so on.

Selection responses are widely used to reflect attitudes or opinions on rating scales, for example, rating the reliability of a car:

Question: *Please look at this card. From* **a** *to* **d** *how do you rate the reliability of your present car?*

a very satisfactory; **b** satisfactory; **c** unsatisfactory; **d** very unsatisfactory.

A weakness of these scales is that (on their own) they give no idea of underlying reasons, but they also tend to show a response bias (the more negative levels of the scale are less often used and so fail to make a distinction). You can overcome this by using a *forced choice* format. If the research is to determine priority features in car purchase, for example, you might do it as follows:

Question: From this list *(show card)* **a** to **g** which is the *most* important feature when you are choosing a car *(pause for response)*; and which is the *least* important?

a   rear passenger doors
b   fuel economy
c   luggage space
d   safety features
e   ease of parking
f   rapid acceleration
g   range of colour options

A common way of assessing attitudes is to provide show cards bearing statements such as: *International level footballers are paid too much even allowing for their entertainment value*, to which the respondent is asked: *Do you agree or disagree with this statement?*

Restricted though the range of question/answer formats may be, they are capable of considerable variation in use, so that one can obtain a lot of information, of a 'surface' categorical kind, very quickly. Essentially such data provide a *descriptive* rather than an *explanatory* picture.

Presentation of findings

Because the data resulting from a closed choice format are effectively *pre-coded* or *pre-analysed,* as with the self-completed questionnaires, then the results for the interviews as a group are easily displayed as *descriptive statistics*, that is in terms of ranges, proportions or frequencies (see Chapter 20).

To recap: there are three categories of data:

- subject descriptors
- self-reported behaviours
- attitudes/opinions/judgements.

The first of these may be in terms of a *quota*, for example, approximately equal numbers of men and women over 45 years. If we have data on socio-economic status, derived from information about present or previous employment, then we can further sub-divide along this dimension, perhaps according to a manual/non-manual distinction.

This is *quantitative* analysis in terms of simple descriptive/count criteria. But when you can sort people (and their responses) into different categories (men v. women for example), you can carry analysis a stage further, looking to see whether men and women (as groups) give different answers to the same questions.

Inferential statistics

We shall make no more than passing mention here of techniques which are described more fully in Part IV.

Answers to closed questions, as in self-completed questionnaires or recording schedules, despite their other limitations are suited to an analysis of *differences* between different categories of respondent. If we take the question about the earnings of top-level footballers we might find the following data as shown in Table 11.1.

On balance, women appear more likely than men to agree with the statement that footballers are paid too much: there *is* a difference in terms of simple numbers. What inferential statistics (those concerned with drawing an *inference* from the data) allow us to do is to specify whether it is probable that this difference could have arisen by chance (note that any difference can arise by

Table 11.1 2 × 2 contingency table for chi square analysis

	Agree	Disagree	Totals
Male	20	40	60
Female	40	35	75
Totals	60	75	135 = N

chance, but it is a matter of greater or lesser probability). The relevant test of significance here is called *chi square* – a so-called non-parametric or 'small-sample' statistic (see pp. 151–2). The importance of this kind of test is that it can head you off from making unwarranted assumptions about an observed 'difference', or alternatively support your judgement.

Combining different kinds of interview data

We have compared recording schedules with questionnaires. But they must also be seen as a source of one kind of data in comparison with other kinds of interviews, in particular those concerned with a more in-depth, qualitative approach, to which they can add a descriptive and possibly 'representative' dimension.

Note that the construction of a representative sample involves an understanding of *survey* techniques, beyond the scope of the present book: Chapter 8 in Robson (2002) is recommended for this purpose. This social survey approach can provide an indication of differences within the group of interest which could then be explored via focus group or semi-structured interviews. If, for example, the data difference shown in Table 11.1 proves to be statistically significant, then a further question would be *why* there is this gender difference. These issues, among others are discussed in Chapters 20 and 22.

Summary

Positives

- quick to administer;
- overcomes disadvantages of postal questionnaires;
- analysis is straightforward.

Negatives

- restricts coverage;
- data are often superficial.

12 The video interview

Some of us are old enough to remember when video was an exciting new tool for researchers in the social sciences, particularly in the area of social interaction, and especially where the interactions were largely non-verbal. Because it allows a repeated review of the same visual sequence, you are enabled to see the fine-grained elements of these interactions, and their complexity.

I can recollect sitting with a PhD student who was researching mother–baby interaction, focusing on the analysis of sequences of *mutual imitation* – one of the earliest forms of communication. The student played through an edited section of the tape several times; at first I couldn't 'see' what was going on. But gradually, and then quite clearly, I did.

There is, of course, a big difference in the communicative capacity of a six-month-old baby with its mother, and two adults in an interview situation. But non-verbal aspects of communication between people who are talking to each other are an important, because qualifying, aspect of the meaning of what is being said.

What is lost in audio recording and transcription?

By definition, an audio recording loses those aspects of communication which are non-verbal, which means that a layer of meaning is stripped out. But the process of transcription removes another layer: those paralinguistic features such as tone, pace and emphasis that further qualify the actual words people are using. Reading the written-word version of an interview, even when faithfully transcribed, you can sometimes feel (especially if you conducted the live interview) that it has somehow been de-natured.

What follows from this is that *a video recording of an interview is the most complete account*, however it is subsequently dealt with.

The video interview as a form of reference

Qualitative research, with its emphasis on the interpretation of data and in the case of interviews, the progression from the actual interview to transcription, to analysis of content, to selection and emphasis in the writing of the research report, is vulnerable to selective reporting. Lincoln and Guba (1985) emphasize the importance of the 'audit trail' to demonstrate the *trustworthiness* of the process by which the research conclusions are reached. In back-tracking through the process, with a video recording you can return to the starting point of the interview, as it actually happened, asking the question: is the research report a valid, if edited, representation of this?

Other positive features of the video interview

A problem with audio recordings, even of good quality, is that unless they are transcribed almost immediately after the interview it may be difficult to recognize what is being said: recent memory helps this recognition. We noted earlier the practical point that it is easier to hear and recognize what people are saying if you can *see* them saying it. This aid to recognition is even more important when the video recording is of a focus-group interview: if you can *see* a person speaking, you can *hear* them more clearly. And, in that context, you can of course *identify* the speaker. For this reason, immediate transcription, although desirable, is not essential when you have all the additional visual information to support your listening.

Setting up a video interview

Today's video equipment is smaller, of better visual and audio quality, and easier to use: it is also less expensive in real terms. But it is more trouble to set up than other forms of recording; and its use depends upon its being readily available. In a university department whose research involves human subjects that is likely to be the case.

A suitable room is another matter; it needs to be convenient for both interviewer and interviewee(s) *and* the recording equipment. The ideal is a dedicated video recording studio or something that passes as such. It should go without saying that those being interviewed should have been informed, and have *agreed* to the procedure prior to the interview.

Checking as to picture and sound quality is a preliminary not to be neglected; and this should be preceded by a practice session with a colleague so that the researcher has the details well worked out (position of chairs, operation of equipment, and so on).

Does video recording affect the behaviour of those being filmed?

Unless the interviewee (and, perhaps, the interviewer) are practised video per- formers or have become inured to the medium, the answer is likely to be 'yes'. The effect is hard to gauge and varies greatly from one individual to another. Audio recording equipment (less obtrusive anyway) is soon ignored; the seeing eye of a camera is another matter. Even if they have agreed, when it comes to it, the person being interviewed might feel so uncomfortable ('exposed' was the word one interviewee used to me) that it would clearly be wrong to pro- ceed. It is essential to be able to offer the alternative (which should be to hand) of a simple audio recording; otherwise they may feel that they have let you down, another complication in the complex character of social relations. Note that it is up to the *researcher* to look out for signs of this discomfort and to take the initiative in raising the issue and dealing with it.

A more general effect, again hard to specify, but real enough impression- istically, is that people (including the researcher) are more conscious of being 'performers'. Only sometimes does this appear to affect the content or quality of what is said but any such apparent effects (and the presumed reasons for these) need to be noted.

The uses of video recording interviews

1   *For training and presentation purposes*
    Training interviewers, in any context, is difficult because it devolves very much on skills that are seen as part of the person. Seeing yourself in this detached way and 'analytically' is, initially, difficult to the point of being traumatic. But accommodation to this reality is part of becoming a skilled interviewer; and video undoubtedly has a part to play in this.

    A demonstration video showing the use of particular techniques that are hard to describe (like *reflecting*, see pp. 35–6) is also valuable, especially if the video shows the tutor (not *too* expert, ideally) who then has the status of a prophet in his own country. Students seeing me having to work at it appears to be a comforting experience.

    The use of the video of an actual interview for training or other presentation purposes such as a conference report has a quite differ- ent potency. Anyone being interviewed obviously has to agree to the recording (or clips from it) being used for this purpose. They should be offered the opportunity to view what you propose to use, as well as being clear as to what kind of audience will see it and why. They should also be told of the probable 'life' of the recordings, that is, at what point they will be destroyed.

2   *For research interview development purposes*

In the same way that inexperienced interviewers can improve their general skills by watching themselves on video, so the researcher can improve their interview schedule (and their use of it) by making a video of a 'pilot' interview as a part of the process of refinement.

It can then be analysed in different ways:

(a) The *skills* level, as detailed in the self-observation questionnaire on pp. 31–2.

(b) The working of the *schedule* itself: general impressions, or notes taken during the interview may miss elements because your attention was on managing the detail of the interview as it happened. Watching it later as a semi-detached observer, you see elements that are redundant, or out of sequence, or don't quite work as intended.

(c) Thinking in terms of the 'audit trail', a recording such as this is part of the chain of evidence of *how* the research procedures have been developed.

3   *For recording complex group interviews*

As noted in Chapter 9, any kind of recording of a group interview is difficult, because of the 'confusion' factor and the multiple elements that have to be attended to. In a focus group interview the round-the-table grouping can be adapted to a 'horseshoe' arrangement with the video recorder facing the group and the facilitator being at one end of the horseshoe configuration.

A video recording which can be replayed and analysed progressively, also allows for a more complete *description* of the pattern of interaction, which can be complex as well as fast-moving. That participants tend to adopt a more courteous, turn-taking style of interaction means some loss of spontaneity but it does make transcription and analysis a great deal easier.

4   *For micro-analytic purposes*

The complexity of an interview is more than the different 'layers' of meaning mentioned earlier. The fine detail of interaction, perhaps of more interest to sociolinguists, also becomes available. Here we are in the realm of *conversation analysis* which is beyond the remit of this book, but warrants mention. An introduction to this is provided by Myers (2000) in a chapter which is particularly well-referenced, in addition to providing guidance on further reading.

5   *As a means of presenting narrative or thematic interview data*
A particular kind of challenge is the analysis and presentation of narrative interview data: how can one manageably, but validly, present the 'story' the interviewee is telling? By definition, these kinds of interviews are not analysed in a tidy categorical sense, although a compromise is possible.

In practice, it is often more satisfactory to attempt both: a broadly categorized analysis which enables the researcher to present key elements from such interviews; and either a textual narrative written almost like a short story as is suggested on pp. 127–8 or an edited version of the video interview which conveys the 'live' quality of the narrative.

The challenge for analysis and interpretation is to reduce and organize the raw data to make them more accessible, and to ensure that the reduction is a fair representation.

6   *As a component in a case study or survey*
Case studies aim to represent a contextualized social phenomenon, whether an individual, group or institution, by the use of multiple sources of data available in the actual setting. Interviews can be one of these sources, and if seen as illustrative and complementary, can make a distinctive contribution to the *range* of data. In the case of a large-scale survey which aims to be representative but where the main report is abstract, summary and general, interview data are most potent when they are 'live' and used to illustrate some of the general conclusions drawn from the survey.

7   *As part of a structured observation/experiment*
There are some kinds of interview (see the next chapter) which are a combination of *observing* what the subject is doing (for example, trying out a piece of new technological equipment) as well as asking questions about it. Only video will allow you to record both dimensions and to engage in the kind of detailed scrutiny and analysis required. Note that both elements contribute complementary aspects of the data needed for the research purpose.

The role of video in a research report

The academic convention is that a research report is essentially textual in form: supplemented perhaps by tables, figures and occasionally by illustrations. Digital technology and related media are changing that and challenging the very nature of how data are presented and academic arguments formed.

Video was a forerunner of the new media. In the domain of interviewing and in research which focuses on these methods, there is a case to be made for the inclusion of such a medium, at least in a research degree submission. As information technology advances, becomes more flexible and less expensive, video and digital data, suitably analysed, could have greater potential in research reporting.

Summary

Positives

- the most complete record of an interview;
- allows various forms and levels of analysis;
- easier to 'hear' what is said and identify speakers in a group.

Negatives

- requires a suitably equipped room;
- interviewees can feel 'exposed';
- camera consciousness may encourage 'play acting'.

13 The interview as a qualitative experiment

Research *methods* are devised to meet the needs of research – to answer particular questions. What makes research so demanding is that you cannot always rely on 'off-the-shelf' techniques but frequently have to adapt them to fit a specific topic. And sometimes you have to devise something new (as far as you know).

What is described here are some simple techniques intended to meet the needs of research students in the area of design – specifically textiles and product design. Although developed for these purposes, one can see that they constitute approaches of wider application in any context where someone is showing a 'product' and asking, essentially: *what do you think?* Such approaches can also be combined with *structured observation*: that is, watching what people do as well as listening to their views and commentary.

What is an experiment?

True experiments are the province of the natural sciences but the social sciences often adopt their methodology which, when used in this way, commonly has its own peculiar difficulties and characteristics (chemical elements don't try to interpret or second guess what is going on as human subjects do). But the analytic style and precise procedures, with the promise of disentangling complex elements of behaviour, constitute a powerful appeal, even when the application is problematic.

But what exactly is a classic experiment in human terms? This is best answered by taking an example which involves people but where physiological measures are also involved. Let us assume that the purpose of the research is to evaluate the effects of a new drug on blood pressure levels. A large number of people (hundreds if not more) who suffer from varying degrees of hypertension are randomly assigned to an *experimental* group and a *control* group. Random allocation distributes individual characteristics so that the groups are comparable. The experimental group is given the new drug, the control group is given a placebo: this is the *independent* variable that is manipulated. Neither the patients, nor the medical researchers administering the drug or placebo, nor those evaluating the results know who has been given which. This is known as a *triple-blind* study to eliminate expectation factors (most importantly in the patients themselves).

Blood pressure level measured before and after the trial period is the *dependent* variable: that on which the independent variable (drug or placebo) is presumed to have an effect (or not) as the case may be.

Human judgements and preferences have effectively been factored out though, needless to say, some of those in the placebo group will have shown dramatic improvements which require other kinds of explanation (having one's blood pressure taken in the context of a rigorous scientific experiment may be a sobering experience and lead to changes in lifestyle). But what relevance has this kind of experiment here?

The notion of structured comparison

Even when a classic experiment is not feasible or appropriate, you can still adopt (and adapt) some of the virtues of what is, essentially, a form of structured comparison. Designers, like other practitioners such as teachers, nurses, or administrators, are often 'experimenting' in the sense of trying things out, following up lines of enquiry, forming judgements. Sometimes these processes would benefit from being carried out, and reflected upon, more systematically. For example, designers always seem to be hurrying on to the finished 'product' which they anticipate will satisfy aesthetic and functional criteria. Sometimes this ends up successfully, quite often it does not. But the underlying reasons are rarely explored other than incidentally or superficially. Success is often attributed to 'flair' or 'intuition' or some such non-explanation.

Being more systematic can mean that one learns more from this process which can also lead to unexpected discoveries. 'Explanations' formed on the basis of careful scrutiny and exploration of *process* and *outcome* constitute the essence of research.

A practical example

Product design has to meet a number of criteria if it is to be successful in the market place, for example:

- functional efficiency;
- value for money;

- aesthetic considerations;
- market appeal.

These are often at variance and their priority is a reflection on the quirks of human psychology. Phillipe Starck's famous lemon squeezer is a good example of a 'successful' product that doesn't meet the first two criteria, but manifestly does meet the last two which are the more difficult to assess because they rest on individual judgement, values and interpretation.

A textile designer with, perhaps, six or seven different design samples might ask a panel of others similarly qualified to rank the samples separately in both *aesthetic* terms and in terms of their *market appeal*.

There is a particular approach to the systematic allocation of ranks: the panel is asked to identify the highest and lowest preferences first – that fixes the end points – then the next in rank order working from both ends (the next highest, next lowest ranking). If you've started with seven, that reduces the unplaced designs to three, which they are then asked to rank in order. This last step is the most uncertain because the assessors may want to rank two the same (and, of course, that can happen earlier); in that case you average the ranks. For example if they can't decide which is fourth and which is fifth, then both are ranked 4.5 (four plus five divided by two). Ranks can be subjected to quantitative analysis in various ways – *displaying* the results but also exploring differences: in the example given, the relationship between the judgements of the designers according to the two different criteria (see Chapter 20).

What has this to do with interviewing? The panel members have made their judgements. You then ask them: *why?* This open question you will need to explore, probing appropriately.

If you employ different panels you can expect they will come up with different rankings because of their different perspectives; and it is a matter of research interest to find these out, and to uncover the reasons. A common discrepancy is one between designers and users, although in some areas of design research the process is much more user-led, as in the next example taken from an area which involves observation combined with interview techniques (and often the use of video).

Interviewing and practical trialling

Inclusive design, which tackles the wider social issue of how product design may *exclude* sections of the population – particularly the mildly disabled and the elderly – has achieved recognition as being key to safety and independence. It is tackled in various ways but essentially involves looking at what people *do* when they use products and what they have to *say* about them. This is an instance where video recording, and observational as well as interview analysis, are exactly complementary in achieving the research aims.

A practical example is the problem that safety bottle caps can present to elderly people with arthritic hands or muscular weakness and, perhaps, defective eye sight. Designed to prevent young children from opening containers of potentially harmful substances, these safety caps usually require a combination of:

- precise positioning of the cap;
- squeezing at appropriate points;
- simultaneously applying downward pressure.

Resolving the difficulties these may present to the elderly requires a detailed exploration of what is involved by analysing a visual recording: gaining insight and understanding from the subjects' commentary and their attempts at the necessary manipulations. Note that simply interviewing users is not adequate, first, because they may not be able to analyse the problems verbally, and second, because a design solution needs the designer's eye on the evident difficulties involved. This combination of evidence touches on the frequent need for *multi-method approaches* (dealt with in Chapter 22).

The role of demonstration linked to exploratory interviewing is applicable across a wide range of professions and not just to products but also *procedures*. Researchers in a practical context need to be alert to different ways of collating evidence; ensuring a flexible attitude of mind as to what could be collected or looked for. Recording a demonstration can be a problem but one can accumulate, for example, sketches of artefacts, or other samples. And increasingly, the use of compact digital cameras means that one can obtain a quick visual record in a notebook fashion.

Summary

Positives

- combines complementary interview and observational data;
- judgements can be subjected to quantitative display and analysis;
- demonstration prompts interview questions.

Negatives

- recording visual components can be difficult;
- collating a range of evidence is time-consuming.

PART III
Distance Methods

14 The telephone interview

The telephone interview has mushroomed as a survey technique in market research since the 1970s, and procedures and analysis here are well developed, see, for example, the standard text *How to Conduct Telephone Surveys* (Bourque and Fielder 2002). The primary emphasis is on the use of relatively brief structured interviews, the results of which can be analysed in a standardized format. But this is an area where market research techniques do not convert well to the purposes and criteria of academic research, particularly where qualitative data are sought.

The technique has sometimes been seen as a means for academic researchers to combine the virtues of survey sampling (where some variant of random sampling techniques is normally used) and in-depth person-to-person interviewing, that is, achieving both representative breadth and interpretive depth. The reality is somewhat different. For example, Russell (1983) carried out a telephone survey of women in San Francisco to interview them about their experiences of sexual abuse as a child: not the easiest of topics for a 'cold call' survey using random digit-dialling techniques to select households. That she achieved a 50 per cent response rate is remarkable but it made a nonsense of the researcher's attempt to achieve a representative group by probability sampling since the characteristics of those who did not respond were unknown.

This imbalance indicates a major weakness of telephone interviewing: that even with the most skilled and persuasive of interviewers there is likely to be a high refusal rate to 'cold calls'. Telephone interviewers in market research are highly trained to overcome initial resistance including assurances that, for example, 'this will only take five minutes and we would really like to know what you think'.

Some authorities emphasize the use of 'pre-calls' and introductory letters, perhaps indicating topic headings so that the targeted person at least *feels* consulted about participation. See, for example, the book by Frey and Oishi (1995) which deals with these approaches and also seeks to distinguish the criteria for using telephone and 'in person' interviews.

Privacy, intrusion and persuasion

Almost all people have a telephone in their homes; add to this the dramatic expansion in the ownership of mobile telephones, and linked answering services and text messaging facilities. Many people also have a fax facility and even more an e-mail inbox.

The scope, therefore, for unwanted calls and messages is vast: what was once a minor nuisance has come to be seen as a persistent intrusion on privacy with an associated negative build-up. Dealing with this 'resistance' is a major preoccupation in texts on market survey telephone interviewing; though to be fair, there is also an increasing emphasis on prior consultation and agreement, albeit somewhat muted in practice.

But it is more than a matter of an experienced 'nuisance' value, on the one hand, or the challenge of 'resistance', on the other. The issue is one of intrusion on personal privacy and impinges on the matter of informed consent and right of refusal. Unsolicited telephone interviewing, it is suggested, can be seen as a form of harassment; as unacceptable as other forms of unwanted attention and persuasive pressure. In other words, it becomes an ethical issue which at least requires careful scrutiny before being approved as an acceptable technique in academic research. The acceptable limit, it is suggested, is a *request* for such an interview, with clear information; and presented in such a way that a refusal is accepted without demur.

The advantages of telephone interviewing over other distance methods

The primary advantage is clear: because you are talking 'live' to the respondent you can be *reactive*. Misunderstandings can be clarified, cues can be picked up from tone of voice, prompts and probes can be used, and there is *engagement*: a sense of mutual responsiveness which can be highly productive in the quality of the interview content.

Linked to this is the fact that people talk a great deal more easily than they write. Other distance methods (see the next two chapters) require a text response even if it is only in the curiously cryptic language of the e-mail. This is not a matter of 'literacy' although that can be relevant in some groups; just that writing requires more effort than speaking, even if one is very practised. Even for an experienced academic the 5000 words that one might produce in an hour-long lecture is a great deal less trouble than writing a chapter of the same length.

It follows that you get more material in a telephone interview and this is directly related to quality and complexity. And, notwithstanding the 'resistance' factor mentioned above which mainly relates to 'cold calling', there is usually a greater willingness to respond to requests for a telephone interview than to other forms of distance interviewing.

A final point, that relates to the value of distance interviewing in general, is that people can be interviewed anywhere in the world which is accessible by telephone; and with the widespread use of mobile telephones that does mean *almost* anywhere. The only caution here is to consider the convenience of the person you are interviewing (who may well be a key figure in the research). Calculation of time differences is essential as well as checking patterns of working, which may not be conventional by one's own standards.

The disadvantages of telephone interviewing

The main disadvantage is a corollary of the main advantage: you are interviewing 'live' but you cannot see the person (and vice versa). We are still some way from universal 'video call' telephones (3G). So all those non-verbal elements which are a major part of live communication are missing: a layer of meaning stripped out as we have observed earlier.

It isn't just that you miss cues or visual qualification of what people are saying; you also lose much of that empathy, the interpersonal chemistry so vital to generating the motivation and interest of a face-to-face interview, even between strangers. This is probably fundamental to another difficulty that telephone interviewing presents in that it is extremely hard work to keep going. Because interviewer and respondent have only vocal communication to go on, it requires, if anything, even more concentration than a normal interview. And related to that, irrespective of level of structure, an endurable length of time is less, usually much less than with a face-to-face interview. The *how* of telephone interviewing has much to do with overcoming these limitations.

The level of structure in telephone interviews

Telephone interviews are generally of the more structured variety because they are simpler to work that way; such questionnaire-type interviews are shorter and easier to record with pencil and paper. Conversely, the medium is less well suited to the more *un*structured kind of interview where the interviewer has to, unobtrusively, maintain the flow and direction of the respondent. However, we live in an age where relaxed and easy telephone talking – usually, of course, between friends – has become the norm, perhaps owing to the personal accessory status of the mobile phone.

Apart from the probable need for a greater level of structure, there is the need to assume that, *in any case* a telephone interview is going to be shorter than the conventional variety – no more than half-an-hour, at the most. But with the kind of structured interview which involves a recording schedule and closed questions, it could well be as little as ten minutes.

The patience and tolerance of the interviewee can have a lot of do with how far their convenience and willingness have been consulted and considered.

Preparing respondents

Their consent to (and understanding of) what is expected of them, is an ethical requirement. Those who are approached for this purpose need to be consulted as to *when* you can best telephone them (and *where*). They also need to be entirely clear as to *how long* such an interview will last; and you need to keep to this limit. For some people to be telephoned at work is out of the question: the nature of their duties (for example, as a nurse or teacher) may preclude their being able to clear the necessary space in their timetable. A convenient time to telephone them at home depends on personal circumstances: a parent looking after young children won't be able to respond to a lengthy call when there are immediate care demands.

So it is essential to make an appointment time, just as you would for a face-to-face interview. More than that, you should check at the appointed time whether it is *still* convenient; people with busy lives are often subject to unpredictable changes in demand.

It is often helpful to send some written material: perhaps a copy of the recording schedule (in effect, a questionnaire you can talk them through) which may incorporate 'show cards' so that you don't have to recite a long question; or it may be just a list of questions or topics you want them to respond to.

My experience is that if you send information too far in advance it 'goes stale', that is, the interviewee's responses lack spontaneity. If possible, it is better to send this material by fax or e-mail, even quite shortly before your telephone call. The purpose is not for the respondent to 'rehearse' their answers but rather that they should have something visual to refer to so that they are not just dependent on a voice coming down the wire or through the ether, with the strained attention that this seems to involve.

Let us now look at the detail.

The structured telephone interview

As in the face-to-face context (see Chapter 11) a recording schedule involves what is essentially a questionnaire consisting of mainly closed questions, and show cards from which the respondent indicates some of their choices, and replies to simple questions involving no more than a straightforward question and answer (*Have you ever bought furniture from IKEA?*).

The schedule (or as much of it as is necessary for the respondent to see) is in front of them when they are responding. The interviewer has a parallel form on which to record the interviewee's responses. This is the most straightforward kind of telephone interview and the most commonly used.

The semi-structured or unstructured telephone interview

These are often 'key' interviews forming part of the substantive empirical content of a research project. They are usually conducted in this way because the interviewee is not easily accessible geographically; perhaps being hundreds or even thousands of miles away. With key data like these, it is essential to strive for maximum quality.

Even here sending the (mainly open) questions in advance is helpful. The interviewee can see the structure of the interview and doesn't so easily 'lose the place' in their responses. The challenge for the interviewer is to maintain the level of sensitive attention necessary for a productive interview: this means not interrupting because of attempts to record manually what the interviewee is saying. It is technologically straightforward to record both parties in a telephone interview, using equipment from a specialist office supplier. The cost is not great (about £150 in the UK) and is typically capable of recording interviews up to 90 minutes (not that it will take so long). A little practice is necessary but no more than with a conventional audio tape-recorder.

However, the main problem in using telephone-recording equipment is its 'invisibility' with connotations of 'telephone tapping' and other phobias of our present-day society. It is a minimum ethical criterion that interviewees should be informed that the interview will be recorded in this fashion. But people often pay little attention to this information or may not fully appreciate what is meant by 'recorded'. So not only is it essential to get prior agreement, but it is also necessary to *remind* people at the time that recording is taking place.

The interviewee will have the list of questions in front of them; the interviewer will have that plus (in the case of the semi-structured interview) a list of prompts. The list of questions has several functions for the respondent – they can see the structure of the interview, can reflect on the direction of their answers – but they can also 'see' how long the interview will last. To some extent, they can pace themselves so that the duration is partly under their control, lessening that sense of being pinned down by an interviewer in an indeterminate fashion.

A brisk pace is part of the character of a telephone interview; not only does it make for good coverage but it conveys the message that time is not being wasted, and that the respondent's time is valued. The approximate duration of the interview should have been specified in advance anyway.

Otherwise the structure of the interview should be as indicated in the relevant earlier chapters (principally 7, 8 and 10). While less time needs to be devoted to preliminaries – except to check understanding of what is involved – attention needs to be paid to closure. You should ask whether there are any other points the interviewee wants to make; whether they feel satisfied with what they've said; explain what you plan to do with the interview and the research project as a whole. You can check whether they would like to see a transcript of the interview and confirm that you will send a summary of the project's findings. Thus although the 'leave-taking' is nowhere near as protracted as at the end of a face-to-face interview, it should not seem abrupt with the phone going down as if they have been cut off.

Summary

Positives

- can combine virtues of survey sampling and in-depth interviewing;
- has some of the qualities of face-to-face interviewing;
- interviews not bound by geographical distance;
- a range of levels of interview structure possible.

Negatives

- general resistance to 'nuisance' factor i.e. unwanted communications;
- non-verbal elements missing (though this may change);
- duration of interviews limited.

15 The e-mail interview

Sarah Lowndes

The Internet was developed during the 1980s by the US National Science Foundation to provide shared time on supercomputers for American universities and research centres, but with the development of microcomputers of increasing power it has eventually grown to encompass billions of other computer users worldwide.

E-mail (or electronic mail) is a system that allows messages to be sent from and received by personal computers via a computer network or a telephone connection. In tandem with the development of the Internet, e-mail has revolutionized the speed with which information can be transmitted and shared. As the art historian, Oliver Grau writes: 'The scale of recent and current encroachment of media and technology into the workplace and work processes is a far greater upheaval than other epochs have known' (2003: 3). These advances continue to be enormously valuable for researchers in all disciplines, who can now instantly access a wealth of information on-line and take advantage of the speed and flexibility of e-mail as a method of communication.

Applications of e-mail

The e-mail interview has three applications: the main one being when the respondent is too busy to meet or lives in another city or country. In these circumstances, an e-mail interview can create access to people whose testimony would otherwise be difficult to record.

The second important use of the e-mail interview is when it is the preferred option of an interviewee who is reluctant to participate in a face-to-face or telephone interview. When the interview subject is diffident or apprehensive about the pressure to perform articulately in a 'live' situation, the e-mail interview can be offered as an alternative. Less intimate than more traditional interview techniques, it allows respondents to participate from a distance and in their own time; this type of interview is therefore considerably less intrusive. The e-mail interview does not put the subject 'on the spot', as they are able to control both their rate of response and the terms in which their response is made.

Finally, the e-mail interview is an ideal way to clarify minor factual details such as an individual's date of birth or occupation. Many people respond to e-mail messages more rapidly than to conventional letters or messages left on an answering machine. In addition, the request is received in writing but much faster than those sent via traditional post (known as 'snail mail' in e-mail parlance).

In some respects, the e-mail interview combines some of the positive aspects of a face-to-face interview, while avoiding some of the drawbacks associated with more conventional methods. However, the e-mail interview also has several problems, discussed in some detail below, with examples drawn from my recent social history of the Glasgow art and music scene (Lowndes 2003).

Some advantages of e-mail interviewing

Like the face-to-face interview, the e-mail interview can yield good quality data, often 'colourful' material which is quite specific. The informal register of the medium – closer to the telephone call than the letter – yields material that is personal, descriptive and often features examples of colloquial speech. In comparison with questionnaires and observation techniques, an e-mail interview can also provide greater depth and complexity of material.

Moreover, while the conventional face-to-face interview is very time-consuming, both in setting up and conducting the interview and transcribing the recording, the e-mail interview requires considerably less investment of time. It does not have to be conducted in real time; the interviewer needs only to send the questions; and one of the major plus points is that it is 'ready transcribed' – a significant time saving when compared with the traditional interview.

The good interpersonal skills required for the successful face-to-face interview are largely circumvented by the use of e-mail. For example, eye contact and active listening, so important in face-to-face interviews, do not come into play in an e-mail interview situation. However, this is not to suggest that the e-mail interview is without social sensibility: certain unwritten rules govern successful e-mail communication. For example, the use of capitals in e-mail correspondence is generally perceived as akin to shouting in everyday conversation and thus is best avoided.

A more informal register?

People usually express themselves better verbally than they do in writing but there are exceptions: some people are more articulate in writing than they ever are in speech. As has been suggested, diffident or less articulate individuals may welcome the opportunity to re-read and edit their responses. However, sometimes the tidy nature of the e-mailed response does not stand comparison with the engaging candour of remarks made spontaneously within the context of a successful face-to-face interview.

Speech and writing are two different forms of language: speech being traditionally seen as guarantor of presence and authenticity, with the written word constituting a comparative sense of artifice and of absence. (A more elaborated and sophisticated exposition of this idea can be found in Derrida 1976.)

An e-mail correspondence, however, often produces a sense of 'telepresence' – a term derived from virtual reality, describing the sensation of feeling in a different place or time afforded by certain technologies. As new media theorist Rachel Greene explains, 'telepresence' is a characteristic of much Internet behaviour, in the way that reading an e-mail from an overseas friend produces a kind of intimacy that belies geographical distances (Green 2004). This sense of immediacy is even more pronounced in the e-mail 'conversations' facilitated by virtual chat-rooms, where real-time e-mail exchanges can take place between two or more participants.

Despite the immediacy of Internet-based communications and the informal register associated with e-mail, it should still be regarded as a more considered form of expression than 'unguarded' spontaneous speech. In an interview situation, people will often exaggerate or recall certain facts incorrectly. The common tendency to over-emphasize the importance of their role in given events may be more pronounced in e-mailed responses, where interviewees may be especially conscious of portraying themselves favourably. As with other research methods, cross-referencing is essential to ensure accuracy.

Another problem is that subjects will often respond in a manner that is similar to speech, but distinguished by the use of forms of punctuation such as exclamation marks, inverted commas, parentheses and phrases such as 'etc.' or 'et al.', which do not appear in normal speech. The two examples given demonstrate this tendency:

> *Eventually, this frustration with 'knowing too much' led me to try and examine what it was that I really did know about the place that I considered 'mine'.*

Very generally I do perceive an increased emphasis on formal concerns, more painting and less work which is obviously 'issue'-based (a term which now sounds very dated!).

While some responses to e-mailed questions may be rather stilted, at the other end of the spectrum are the responses that are so chatty and idiomatic that they are not really useful in the context of a serious piece of research. The tendency to informality in the e-mailed response is linked to the speed at which e-mails are received and read and responses returned. This speed carries with it a frisson of excitement: hitting the 'send' button means that the words are dispatched with a kind of finality. Once sent, they cannot be taken back or qualified as they could be in a face-to-face or telephone conversation.

The 'virtual' nature of Internet exchanges means that responses sent in e-mails may be more playful or flippant than ideally one would wish. The difficulty here seems to be encouraging the interviewee to view your questions as different in intention and tone from the numerous other light-hearted messages that may fill their inbox. Here is an example of a rather too informal response:

Also she has been great at providing us with the space and then giving us the freedom to arrange and curate things, quite unusual as I am sure a lot of people would want more of their say . . .

Sometimes e-mailed responses will contain humorous abbreviations and phrases typical of the e-mail lexicon, such as TMI (too much information). As with the text-messaging phenomenon, much is lost in the condensation of sentiments: 'LVU!' seems considerably less romantic than 'I love you', for example, though the phrase is unlikely to feature in your research project. The drive towards increased speed creates both a sense of urgency and a lack of serious intent.

Similarly, people responding to e-mailed questions have a tendency to use abbreviations, or to express themselves in notation form or to list information rather than describe it fully, for example:

More affordable studios, more resources/info about: courses, exhibiting spaces, where you can access equipment or materials, openings etc.

Residencies, fellowships etc. are one means but often very demanding on time and of course may mean relocation/time away from home and/or studio which can be detrimental at certain stages in anyone's practice.

Often it will be possible either to ask the interviewee to expand further or (with their agreement) to adjust such responses to make them more readable. When providing references for such quotations, it is important to specify that they derived from e-mail interviews and were not arrived at 'in conversation' – thus accounting for any unevenness in tone.

Another potential problem of the e-mail interview is that it carries a risk of misinterpretation. The emotional tenor of an e-mail can be hard to read, which has led to the popular use of smiling faces, winking faces and sad faces, composed of colons, semi-colons and brackets, to indicate when the author is being humorous, ironic or genuinely serious [:) ;) : (].

Speed and flexibility

Despite various drawbacks associated with the e-mail interview, this method has two over-riding advantages, namely the speed and flexibility of the form. As Michael Benedikt, editor of the book *Cyberspace*, writes: 'In patently unreal and artificial realities ... the principles of ordinary space and time can be violated with impunity' (1992: 128). What this means in terms of the inter-viewer/interviewee relationship is that enquiries and responses can be posted and received outside office hours and in a variety of locations (at work, at home, in hybrid home/work spaces like hotels, airports and Internet cafés). Very busy individuals, who might be reluctant to commit themselves to physi-cally meeting for an hour, may be willing to devote more time to composing an e-mail response which they work on as and when it suits them. Often the respondent will be willing to clarify or expand upon certain points in a follow-up e-mail. Occasionally, a back-and-forth dialogue may develop which yields considered, in-depth responses.

Recommended approaches

Perhaps more than any other approach described in this book the e-mail interview is best used as one of a range of methods: different styles of inter-view, observation, documentary search and analysis, the collection of artefacts (see Chapter 22).

As with all other kinds of interviewing, it is essential to research the sub-ject thoroughly beforehand, both to make the interview worthwhile for the researcher, and as a mark of respect for the interviewee. If the interviewee is someone of high professional standing, they may be more willing to answer your questions if these have an original perspective and differ in some import-ant respect from questions they have been asked by previous interviewers (see also Chapter 8: The Élite Interview).

After you have received an initial positive response to your e-mail inter-view request, it is necessary to be clear about the timeframe you are working to.

This means providing a specific date within which you would like to receive a reply: most people respond better to this than a vague 'hope to hear from you soon'. And as an e-mail is considerably less intrusive than a telephone call, it is also not at all inappropriate to politely remind respondents that you are still waiting to hear from them.

Summary

Positives

- instant communication access worldwide;
- acceptable to those reluctant to participate in a face-to-face interview;
- extremely economical on time;
- response is at interviewee's convenience;
- no transcription required.

Negatives

- responses can be too colloquial for research purposes;
- responses can be very abbreviated or edited;
- e-mails can accumulate or be ignored.

16 The 'open' questionnaire interview

At the beginning of Chapter 1 we attempted to define an interview and, from that definition, to distinguish it from a questionnaire. Exceptions were noted but the distinction largely applies. In the present chapter, however, that distinction will be qualified for practical purposes.

We have emphasized the variety of ways in which a researcher can obtain information and insight from people; and the need to think flexibly about what precise methods would be feasible or suitable in a given situation. To a large extent these vary according to the availability or characteristics of the interviewee, who is often selected as representative of a larger group and, in that respect, replaceable. But sometimes the people one might want to interview are neither particularly accessible nor replaceable. Hence the importance of 'distance' techniques or those which make only limited demands; or both. Here we describe two variants of a simple technique that will suit some respondents and some purposes.

Questionnaires are normally composed of *closed* questions with various forms of multiple-choice answer. Because these answers are 'pre-coded' – that is, already defined in categorical terms – they are easy to analyse in a standardized format and thus are appropriate for the very large number of responses possible in a large-scale survey. The experienced social researcher knows that a questionnaire with *open* questions, where the response is open to the respondent's free choice, results in a data set which is almost unanalysable. Even with the use of sophisticated software, it still requires the researcher to 'code' (derive categories from) the data, and with a vast amount of qualitative data that soon becomes a gargantuan task.

Although interviews are normally face-to-face and interactive, a key element is the openness to the possible responses of the interviewee. A 'questionnaire' as described here which asks (normally a very few) open questions lies somewhere between a live interview and a standardized-format questionnaire.

When would one use an open questionnaire interview?

Such a questionnaire interview sent through the post is hardly high tech but it is a long-established 'distance' technique and, if it antedates the telephone and the e-mail, it might on occasion be more acceptable to the potential respondent, and certainly has its own distinctive virtues.

What are these qualities? A simple listing is as follows:

- While the great majority of people are accessible by telephone, and probably most by computer, everyone, apart from the homeless, is accessible by post.
- Something which requires a written response can wait on the convenience of the respondent.
- It allows for a more considered, reflective response; additions, alterations can be made (although this can mean that significant material is edited out).
- It may well suit the *style* of some people – those who, for example, do not like a telephone interrogation or the reflex response of an e-mail.

And finally:

- Because the response is written, it will usually be more succinct than speech; and no transcription is required.

The main disadvantage is that not everyone is easily literate and, even when they are, may not like making an extended written response: it does involve more work. Even if this is the respondent's preferred option (you give a choice, obviously), the number, and range, of questions should make the task as easy as possible for them. This means that *only key questions are asked* which entails prioritizing: what is it that you really need to know from this particular person?

Number of questions and length of response

Quite simply the longer the answer you anticipate, or require, the fewer the questions. Related to this is the outer boundary of how long anyone can reasonably expect a 'written' response to be. There is no algorithm for this apart from the dictates of common sense. My own experience is that a *total* length of three A4 pages is a not-too-daunting requirement. And how many questions?

Something between three and six is another rule-of-thumb guide; that is to say, three questions with a page each, or six with half-a-page for each response. The latter usually appears to be the more acceptable. A full-page response looks a good deal more demanding and may be proportionally more discouraging.

How open should the questions be?

The distinction between open and closed questions is one of degree as much as kind: there are grades of openness. You can narrow the focus of possible responses by the way the question is framed; and if in terms of space the response is expected to be 'economical', then it is as well to ensure that this economy is not wasted.

In a face-to-face interview you can ask an initial wide-open question, and then prompt if specific sub-areas are not covered. In a questionnaire interview these 'sub-topics' may make up the specific questions themselves. For example, in a conventional interview you might have as a question: *What are your views on shopping for food from supermarkets as against smaller, individual stores?* with the following prompts to be brought in if the topics are not covered spontaneously:

- convenience of one-stop shopping and parking;
- use of local shops/markets;
- range/quality/price of goods;
- specialist shops;
- 'ethnic' food stores;
- sources of organic food stuffs.

In a questionnaire interview these could be turned into six separate questions. Or you could turn each of them into a total topic, asking further sub-questions, and so on. How far you focus the questions gives a greater or lesser degree of openness. That is, the response is more or less *indicated*.

Question and topic preparation has been covered, as a general issue, in Chapter 3. Its importance in the present case is that the scale of the response is restricted by the medium. *Piloting* should be carried out as with any other interviewing variant: the point being that a certain amount of 'slack' can be accepted in a live interview, but in a questionnaire interview it becomes a major waste of the information-collecting resource.

As in a semi-structured interview, well-targeted questions are not only more productive, they are also more stimulating to the respondent in that you get a more vigorous response.

The audio-tape variant

Audio-tape recordings have been around for so long that their unique and useful characteristics are sometimes overlooked. They are one of the ways in which people geographically far apart can keep in touch: they are live, and personal, and can be replayed at will. Tapes are cheap and can be sent cheaply all over the world via airmail; although, as a personal accessory, a voice tape-recorder is no longer as common as it once was, or is not used as such.

For research interviewing purposes it is a simple matter to send a question sheet and perhaps show cards or illustrative material together with an audio-tape, which can itself include the researcher's introductory remarks.

The main advantages are that it is a medium which overcomes the 'writing' barrier; it allows people to record their views in response to the questions in a way which gives more, and possibly richer, material. It is one more variant; and one where the respondent has freedom of response, *saying as much as they want.*

Ensuring prompt returns

This is largely a matter of common-sense courtesy. The principal points are these:

- Ensuring that the material arrives at a time which is convenient for the respondent (and this may mean sending it by some form of express or special delivery).
- Enclosing a return envelope (a padded one in the case of tapes) with the appropriate postage – perhaps for a secure delivery rate. Requests that go overseas should be accompanied by International Reply Coupons which cover the postage costs from anywhere in the world.
- Indicating when you would ideally like the material returned – explaining this in terms of your data collection and analysis timetable.
- Using a prompting phone call – ostensibly to check that the respondent has received the material.

It is not claimed that the content of a questionnaire interview matches in interpretable quality the kind of detailed insights that are possible from a semi-structured interview. Like other abbreviated media it is a way of getting key data from a source that is not readily accessible by any other means.

Summary

Positives

- a way of reaching almost everybody;
- can provide key data cheaply;
- can 'wait' for attention;
- may suit some respondents better than 'immediate demand';
- no transcription required (except when an audio recording is made).

Negatives

- not reflexive/interactive;
- makes demands on literate expression (unless audio-taped);
- number of questions and length of response limited.

PART IV
Analysis and Interpretation of Content

17 Transcribing the interview

Transcription is the process of producing a valid written record of an interview: would that it were so simple. It is easy to understand that the stage of data analysis is a selective, interpretive business. It is less easy, until you get down to the practicalities of the task, to appreciate that 'simple' transcription is itself a process of interpretation. Interestingly, the considerable improvements in voice recognition software since the mid-1990s have brought home to us just how interpretive 'straightforward' listening to the human voice is. As with narrative competence (see p. 48), listening in the active sense is a distinctively human characteristic whose precise operation is elusive, at least at the level of software reconstruction. Transcription, in a word, is a form of *translation*.

What is lost in transcription?

The most obvious loss is in the semantic properties of the human voice: those dimensions of speech (emphasis, pace, tone) which can radically alter what the words mean. That is easily appreciated in common-sense terms; reflecting them at the level of transcription is another matter. When the qualification of meaning is very clear, then some observation on the *way* the words were said (as in a play script) will be necessary. Incidentally, this interpretive qualification is one reason why the original tapes should be available as part of the chain of evidence.

Of course there are other features of speech which have a more specialized significance – hesitation phenomena, for example – another area of research for linguists. Analysis in terms of the minutiae of social interaction (as in ethnomethodology) is another dimension but less relevant to the analysis of the substantive detail of interviews.

Where transcription is not needed

Where the basic data are textual (as in e-mail interviews) then there are no features of speech to be lost. What the respondent (presumably) intended is there in the written/printed word. But even here there are levels of meaning, latent conventions of expression, which could be extracted: this kind of 'reading between the lines' is the province of the technique – if it can be called that – of *discourse analysis*. This is beyond the scope of our present purposes but a useful introduction is given by Gill (2000).

Partial transcription is sometimes appropriate, particularly where the interviews are being used to develop a schedule or a questionnaire, that is, where they have a preparatory role in identifying topics and questions, or indicating an appropriate form of words. Here one snatches out of the flow those substantive elements which will be used in the main empirical study.

Selective transcription can also be used with supplementary interviews, once the main categories of analysis have been derived from full transcriptions of earlier interviews. What you find is that the first few interviews throw up most of the categories you derive, and that subsequent interviews add *content* but little in the way of new categories. There comes a point, with the later interviews, where it is more economical to listen for new or additional exemplar statements to include under these category headings, and to transcribe only those. By then you will know what you are looking for, and it can be excessively expensive of time to carry out full transcriptions, yet the substantive content is expanded.

Couldn't computer software do it for you?

We all share a naïve faith in computers, particularly that they will take over the donkey-work of research. They are unbeatable in the area of the organization, storage and retrieval of vast amounts of information. Those of us who can remember the days of pre-computer literature searches have cause to be thankful for the speed and coverage of the major databases, but even here it is the interpretive use of key words that is critical. And it is this element of flexibility, at several levels, which often shows up the limitations of computer software (and the importance of the skilled human interpreter of the system).

Speech recognition software has improved since the 1990s but this has had the effect of making the limitations clearer. What the software does is adapt to your own voice – as if you were 'training' it – but it cannot cope with multiple voices and becomes disorganized. Thus any assumption that widely available software (such as IBM's ViaVoice) will transcribe your interview audio-tapes for you is unrealistic. In practice, what is usually necessary is for the researcher to listen to the tape through headphones and then dictate what they hear, phrase by phrase and clearly and distinctly, into the word processor microphone. This is quite a tedious business and even so, the software makes mistakes in interpretation which have to be corrected. Unless you are fluent in the use of the software, it is hardly a practical option.

Couldn't someone else do it?

Well, they *could*, but there are drawbacks:

- Experienced audio typists, particularly those employed by an agency, are not cheap – perhaps £80–£100 for an hour-long tape, depending on how troublesome it is. (It will take them much longer than an hour.)
- In the same way that it's difficult to analyse an interview you haven't done yourself so it is difficult to hear/interpret it. Whole sections of a tape transcribed particularly via a non-research-sophisticated audio-typist can be garbled, to say the least. In many ways it is unreasonable to expect otherwise.

Doing it yourself is often the only practicable option. If you have conducted the interviews yourself *and* you are a skilled audio touch-typist, it is likely to be the easiest and most efficient way. But only if your keyboard skills are of the effortless variety so that you don't have to think where your fingers are going; all your attention will be needed for listening to what comes through the headphones.

What is the alternative? It is to hand-write the transcription and then either word-process it from that comfortingly static medium or get someone else to word-process it for you, provided your handwriting is legible.

The basic rules for transcription

1 *Do not let the tapes accumulate.* A pile of tapes soon becomes a daunting task: and the longer you leave them, the more difficult transcription becomes.
2 *Transcribe as soon as possible after the interview.* The recency effect will mean that you are able to interpret the recording more easily: your memory will be refreshed by hearing the tape, and assist you in making sense of it.
3 *Ideally transcribe the day after the interview.* It is better to set up a pattern of interview followed by transcription, instead of several interviews followed by several transcriptions. An important aspect of this pattern

is that it allows for learning from one interview to the next. This will have been most rapid at the piloting stage but there are increments from one interview to another. You also need to approach each interview feeling fresh and interested. If you feel the interviews are a slog, this will communicate itself to the respondent.

4   *Be realistic about the time transcription will take.* There is no fast method, even if you get faster with practice. A first transcription of an hour-long tape can easily take ten hours and is unlikely to be less than six. But it is not just a matter of length of time: transcription can be quite stressful because of the level of concentration required.

5   *Don't spend more than an hour at a time on transcription.* Referring to the point just made, if you go on for too long, then transcription quality will suffer. What this means is that the transcription will take not less than a day, and, initially, more than that.

6   *Clearly identify tapes and transcripts.* As a matter of routine you should start each interview with *date* and *name* (or other identifying details) but these should also be clearly labelled on the audiotape, computer disk, and hard copy; and they are best stored together in sets. If you *revise* transcriptions – in terms of revisiting difficult-to-hear sections or changing punctuation patterns – then these drafts should be dated separately and numbered. *In addition, you should always back up your disks.*

Transcription: managing the detail

What exactly do you include in the transcription? It is legitimate to omit the following:

- Most paralinguistic features of speech *unless* they clearly qualify meaning – in which case you insert in brackets a single word to express the mood or emotion (*reluctantly, angrily*).
- Speech hesitations of the *um-er* variety; and other repetitive interjections that add nothing to meaning (I once interviewed someone who said '*You know what I mean?*' almost every other sentence).

What should be included are:

- What the interviewer says as well as the interviewee, but printed in a different font – either italics or, probably better, in capitals so that it marks clearly the sections. In a semi-structured interview it is best to use both: capitals for the main question, italics for the prompts and probes.

- Clear indications of material that is not transcribed because inaudible – usually marked by square brackets [. . .].
- Appropriate punctuation: quite simply, speech is not punctuated other than by pauses and changes in tone and emphasis. These don't translate easily into the conventional notation of written punctuation – particularly full stops and commas. As Lynne Truss demonstrated in her best-selling *Eats, Shoots and Leaves* (2003) these can radically alter meaning. A lack of attention to valid representation via punctuation can result in meaning being scrambled in key passages. Careful listening is necessary to achieve an approximation as to how speech is segmented for meaning. An ellipsis (three or more dots) can be used to show how speech patterns are represented. *Paragraphing* is another aspect requiring interpretive judgement. Using an independent 'interpreter' is useful: at least at the level of taking your transcript and checking it against the audio-tape. In the end it is often impossible to get full agreement – but then punctuation is always to some degree a matter of style and preference.

Reviewing the transcripts

The process of analysis will be covered in the chapters that follow but there is a preliminary stage of checking through your transcripts. First, to see whether you have observed your own conventions from one transcript to another (layout, punctuation, and so on). Standardization here will make analysis easier: typically one finds that later transcriptions fall into more of a pattern than the earlier ones.

The second reason has a quite different purpose although still preparatory in character. You take the hard copies of your transcripts and read them through one after the other rather as you would the chapters of a book. This will give you an overall 'feel' for the content. But it will do something else, and that is to start your mind working on apparent themes or categories – a kind of preparation for the demanding process of interpretive analysis; not a stage to rush into directly after transcription has been completed. If you take a break for a couple of weeks, you will find yourself not just refreshed for the task but mentally ready because of the unconscious work that has been going on.

18 Narrative overview versus categorical analysis

Such a distinction is largely a false opposition: as if in geographical mapping one were forced to make a choice between latitude and longitude. Both are necessary to locate the features which are being identified: in interviewing, the 'horizontal' narrative or the 'vertical' categories within it. These represent different, essentially complementary, approaches; and there is no one *right* form of analysis although how interview data have been gathered can point in one direction rather than another. An unstructured interview is usually conducted with narrative or thematic forms of analysis in mind; a more structured interview indicates a categorical analysis.

What exactly do we mean by 'analysis'? A helpful analogy is to think in terms of the kind of nutritional analysis you see on the side panel of a packet of breakfast cereal. This answers the question: *of what elements is this made up?* which is a kind of categorical analysis. But even at the level of chemical analysis the sum is greater than the parts: the total experience of your cornflakes is not simply an aggregation of the supposedly beneficial ingredients. For one thing, chemicals *in combination* have a different mode of operation than they do in isolation. And so it is with the categorical or thematic elements of a narrative.

To take the analogy further: some elements, even if they do not loom large, are more important or have greater significance than others. Here, of course, the analogy starts to break down. The 'importance' of a chemical element – effect on health for example – is a relatively objective phenomenon. The importance of an element or strand in an interview is a more subjective evaluation: mainly justifiable in terms of how far it helps us to understand what is being studied.

The emergence of significant elements

As noted at the end of the previous chapter the labour of transcription is the beginning of the process of analysis. Nothing takes you so firmly into the detail of the material. Almost unconsciously you start to 'construct' your analysis because intellectual organization does not start out at an explicitly organized level. Indeed, a premature attempt may do violence to the data that have to be assimilated.

When you start the analysis proper, it is important to approach it in a steady, reflective manner, seeing it as a further stage in the emergent process. This is particularly true of narrative analysis: we shall deal with this first to mark its distinction from categorical analysis – and also to demonstrate how one can shade into the other.

An edited or paraphrased account

The validity of a research report of an interview is how faithfully it renders what happened in that interview. Whatever form the analysis takes, a process of data reduction is involved: extracting the essence. Inevitably that means *selection* and *interpretation*, and the one is entailed in the other. Many a politician has complained that an embarrassing quotation has been interpreted 'out of context', with perhaps some justification.

Those of us who can remember doing exercises in paraphrasing or 'précis' at school – reducing some passage to its essential elements – will know what a difficult (and often tedious) business this was. There was often, to say the least, a loss of quality. Attempts to paraphrase an interview can suffer from a similar defect – a kind of deadening of the vivid quality of the live interview. One of the reasons for preserving the words people actually use is that, whether fluent and educated speakers or not, their expression is often compelling; much more so than the bland rendition of an academic researcher.

What is proposed is that the reduction of the narrative strands of an interview is more faithfully represented by an edited version of what the interviewee *actually said* than by a translation into the researcher's words.

Editing the transcript

When people are telling their story, although the broad thrust will be chronological, they will often remember – or see the need to include – elements out of sequence. And there will be repetitions – inevitable (and necessary) in a spoken account, in addition to what can justifiably be called 'padding' – a kind of 'marking time' before moving on. However, the *substantive* elements of an interview (whatever the form of analysis) are not difficult to identify. By substantive is meant those elements which are of substance. Recognizing these is a process more difficult to define than to carry out, and while 'subjective', it is a relatively simple matter to have another researcher marking these elements up as an independent check.

Taking these substantive statements and putting them in chronological order, with a minimum of inter-linking or inserted text from the researcher, is the essence of this task. If it is more art than science, the art lies in selecting direct quotations that *validly* reflect the actual interview: a summary *but in the interviewee's own words*. At the same time one has to avoid the trap of pointing up the interview content by too selective a process of editing. It is a matter of judgement how balanced the end result is. What follows is a section from an interview transcript, followed by the edited version.

Well, it's like a change in the weather, you just know it's going to get worse . . . you didn't actually know. I mean nobody actually said anything . . . I mean we talked amongst ourselves and a lot of . . . rumour, really, but you wonder where it comes from. No smoke without fire. And the atmosphere was different . . . meetings, and things cancelled, and that sort of stuff. Unsettling because nothing was said officially. I asked the Union rep and he said there were discussions ongoing but he'd obviously been told not to say anything . . . All that uncertainty and you start to think: what am I going to do? You get sick of thinking about it . . . and talking . . . I said: let's shut up until we know . . . Days like that, going round and round . . . I stopped going to the canteen; boring it was.

Then they called us all together and . . . well, it wasn't so bad: last in, first out and not reappointing, that sort of thing . . . kind of obvious really.

An edited version involves selection but also the interpolation of a few words to make grammatical sense (conventional when a quotation doesn't make complete sense on its own). These are indicated by square brackets [ ] in the edited version.

You didn't actually know . . . nobody actually said anything. The atmosphere was different – meetings [and so on] were cancelled. [It was] unsettling because nothing was said officially. The Union rep said there were discussions ongoing. All that uncertainty [and] you get sick of thinking about it. [In the end] it wasn't so bad: last in, first out, not reappointing; kind of obvious really.

The extent to which that edited version is satisfactory is a matter of judgement (for example, whether and *how* you indicate omitted material) but the example is clear enough to illustrate the process. But one can see that it does two things:

1   It enables or facilitates further levels of analysis.
2   It provides in a relatively tidy and accessible form a basis for interpret-
    ation, conclusion drawing and theory construction.

How far these further stages are appropriate depends on the use to which the
interviews are put. Where the narrative interviews are complementary to other
kinds of data, for example as illustrative material added on to a social survey,
then they may be sufficient as 'stories' to give a living dimension to large-scale,
representative, but summary data. Such a choice is dictated by the purposes of
the research.

Reducing the data and retaining the meaning

In almost any area of research, 'raw' data – the original, unanalysed accumula-
tion – soon become very substantial. But perhaps nowhere is that more true
than in qualitative research. Interview transcripts, ethnographic accounts,
personal diaries, logs, work process journals, soon assume massive proportions.
Data reduction is essential if the researcher (and those who read the research
report) are to 'see' what is there, whether in a summary, impressionistic fashion
or in greater detail.

There are few tidy and simple rules for identifying key elements, apart
from the dictates of the *purpose* of the research and the particular *questions* that
are being asked. That initial identification is, however, a subjective process, as
seeing meaning always is: there are no formal rules here except the unhelpfully
abstract. No matter how tidy the procedures that follow, they are still dependent on the direction of that first step. The problem in the subsequent stages is
how to retain something of the quality and character of the original data:
which, in the case of interview material, can only be done if the original 'voice'
is retained, that is, *the meanings as expressed by the interviewee.*

But does that not imply, in the case of narrative interviews, presenting
such a mass of material, even when edited (as above) that it can scarcely
be called 'analysis' at all? If we went no further than producing an edited
narrative account that might be fair comment. However, what is proposed
here are forms of further analysis, with linking and interpretive material,
that nonetheless retain essential elements of the original 'voices'. We shall
consider:

*   thematic analysis;
*   stage-structure analysis;
*   categorical content analysis.

Thematic analysis

As described, the totality of an interview transcript can be edited down (to perhaps a third of its original length) by identifying substantive statements and deleting 'padding' and repetition. With some reordering to get the chronological order right and the occasional insertion (which goes in square brackets) to complete or clarify a sentence, you have a valid, accessible approximation to the complete interview. The result is a narrative which is clear, relatively quick to read and yet almost entirely in the interviewee's own words. This process can also be seen as a *first-stage analysis*. That is, it can provide a basis for further reductions or forms of organization.

However, you can also break up a total narrative into particular *themes*, used here in a way which overlaps with other researchers' use of different terms (episodic analysis, critical incident analysis, and so on). What is proposed is a 'cascade' approach: from representing the whole interview in full in an edited format; to identifying themes within it; to carrying out a stage-structure analysis (see below) and, optionally, a narrowly or broadly based categorical analysis – this last dealt with mainly in the next chapter.

What is meant by a 'theme'? In the way it is used here, it is a kind of horizontal category – something that exists as a 'sub-plot' within the main narrative, perhaps dealt with (in a research report) as a section or chapter. Abstracting these subsidiary narratives focuses attention on the structure of the overall narrative. The verbatim example given on p. 128 could constitute an element in a more extended theme on how workers in a factory come to know about threatened job losses: a short story in itself – and in certain circumstances possibly the main focus of a research study.

The defined focus of these sub-plots means that presenting them in series, initially without further reduction, can itself be clarifying to the reader or researcher. But, as with reading a complete account of a narrative interview, it soon becomes apparent that there are levels of abstraction, further stages of analysis that are possible. These are: stage-structure analysis (horizontal); and common-category analysis (vertical).

Stage-structure analysis

In introducing Chapter 7 dealing with 'unstructured' interviews we emphasized that *all* interviews have a structure: in that case constructed by the person being interviewed rather than the researcher. In a given topic area (for example, preparation for retirement) within a narrative one can see *stages* in the account. This identification of stages develops as one works through successive interview transcripts: rather in the way that in developing a categorical analysis the categories derived from a *first* transcript will yield many of those to be found in subsequent transcripts, with each successive transcript adding (progressively fewer) categories. So, in carrying out a stage-structure analysis, one finds that not all respondents fit all the same stages but that there are many common elements which can be represented as a potentially generalizable account.

The stages of a narrative can be as broad or as narrow as one wants but, in preserving the notion of narrative they need to be broad enough to show the progression; and that can be *very* broad, depending on the particular research purpose. I remember as an undergraduate attending a lecture on the contemporary novel by someone in the English Department who said the essence of a novel was people coming together, a problem or conflict, and its resolution – very abstract and summary. But it has stuck in my mind because it was a (simple) framework for understanding what a conventional novel is about. More experimental novels would, doubtless, deny any resolution.

Analysis is about drawing out distinct and potentially *generalizable* features of the data. For the purposes of analysing a narrative interview, it needs to be more detailed than the short-hand example of the structure of the novel.

For example, if we were analysing people's accounts of their progression towards retirement we might extract fifteen stages in more-or-less chronological sequence as in Figure 18.1.

This kind of stage structure is derived inductively from reading through each edited narrative and seeking to identify stages (categories in chronological sequence) which are faithful to the substantive content.

In *writing up* the analysis, each of these stages is treated as a section within the narrative with exemplar quotations from the interviews and linking/ interpretive inserts by the researcher. A more general commentary and summary conclusions follow on from these. The writing up of interview data is dealt with in more detail in Chapter 21 but it is necessary here to indicate how these stages are used.

As well as being used as section headings, the stages shown in the schematic format provide a bird's eye view of the analytic structure; it might also be appropriate to use exemplar quotes within the layout as a 'for instance' illustration.

Of course, these stages have been derived from *all* the accounts so no one interview will evidence each identified stage. It will be necessary to identify how many of the interviewees can be entered in each stage (a simple count frequency); this will then show which are the more substantial components in the structure.

Sometimes it will be the case (depending on the topic and the number of people involved) that *one* stage structure analysis just doesn't fit the range of data: people may have quite different stories to tell. For example, approaches to and experience of retirement may differ radically depending on such variables as gender, occupational class, and so on, in which case they can be grouped and represented differently.

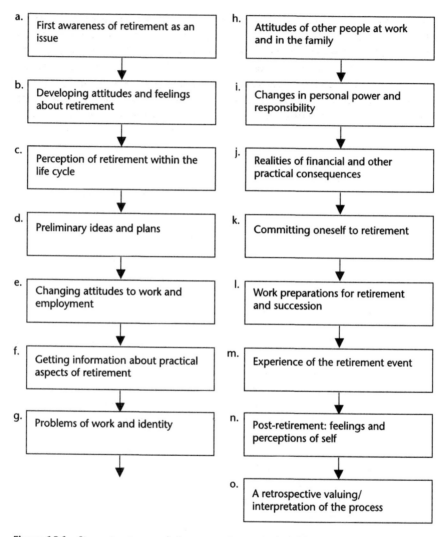

Figure 18.1 Stage-structure analysis: progression towards retirement

Unstructured/narrative interviewing and categorical analysis

Because you have conducted an interview in an unstructured fashion so as to elicit a narrative account, it does not follow that you have to analyse the result in narrative terms. There are many reasons for adopting an unstructured format: it may be that you do not know enough about the possible content to establish a structure, and that some people do not respond well to anything that conveys a sense of control or direction. So you let them tell their story in their own fashion. But if your research *purpose* is concerned with certain elements in their response, when you come to the stage of analysis you fillet out what you want and discard (or put to one side) the rest. In other words, you treat the transcript as if it were the product of a semi-structured interview. Elements will be missing because you weren't able to steer or prompt them but there will also be elements of discovery – things that you had not anticipated and which might have been excluded by a more focused approach.

19 Deriving categories (coding) from the data

Categories are formed in the human mind: they do not exist out there in the external world for us to find. Students, even the art school students I teach, are often worried about the notion of 'subjectivity' because they feel that research should be 'objective' and 'scientific' (*'Isn't that just a subjective judgement?'*). In the sense of being a function of human intelligence *all* judgements are subjective: they could not be anything else. The 'objectivity' lies in making explicit the criteria for the judgement; but the process remains a matter of interpretation and opinion to a greater or lesser degree, and particularly in relation to human behaviour, feelings, opinions, and the like.

In physics and chemistry one comes closest to the notion of objective categories, for example, the periodic table in which the elements are arranged in terms of increasing atomic number. First devised in 1869, the formation of this classification has been progressive, the product of human discoveries and justified revisions. Its value is that it provides a universal basis for understanding and predicting the behaviour of naturally occurring elements. *Agreed* categories are fundamental to these processes of shared knowledge.

Categories and interpretation

There are established procedures for identifying and classifying natural elements; in that sense there is not much scope for 'interpretation'. But if we move to human beings, the picture becomes quite different, even when one is dealing with what would seem to be an objective phenomenon.

The World Health Organization (WHO) has established an agreed classification of the causes of death (the ICD index): there are some 900 main causes of death in this classification. These are used to categorize the mortality patterns of different countries and groups within it (by age, gender, social class, etc.). Death, we can agree, is a relatively objective phenomenon; but deciding the cause(s) of death is another matter. Quite apart from mistakes in post-mortem analyses, there are social and cultural preferences (for example, in relation to suicide); and there are also *fashions* in diagnosis. In the course of researching the area of teenage pregnancies I also reviewed the pattern of infant death. One of the findings was that the incidence of cot death (Sudden Infant Death Syndrome) was significantly higher for babies born to teenage mothers than for babies born to older mothers. But I also found marked differences in the 'use' of this diagnosis. For example, in 1988 almost half of infant deaths in England and Wales were classified as SIDS (ICD 798); whereas in Scotland, for the same year, only around a third of infant deaths were so classified. In both cases there was a rapid decline in these categories in following years. Did these differences and changes in incidence reflect *real* changes in the pattern of causes of infant death? Or were doctors being more cautious in their diagnosis? Probably both, but it makes the essential point: what goes into a category is to a large extent a matter of judgement and interpretation.

Categorizing what people say

Elements of the natural world or causes of death have something in common, even when there are grey areas for classification, since the phenomena are physical and external. But where is the commonality in a set of interviews relating to people's *internal* worlds? In a very real sense, each interview is unique, although this varies according to the amount of structure in the interview.

The main structure is in the questions asked, and how specific or directed they are. Yet even in an unstructured interview you are specifying what it is you want the interviewee to tell you about: in other words, a boundary is set. In a structured interview the category headings are defined by the questions (as in a postal questionnaire) and so are pre-formed – making analysis much easier. What we shall consider here is the categorical analysis of unstructured and semi-structured interviews, however obtained.

'Classic' content analysis

Content analysis originated in the USA at the beginning of the twentieth century as a technique (essentially *quantitative* in character) for analysing the balance of content in newspapers, for example, the proportion of home to foreign news, sports coverage, 'women's pages', and so on. These kind of 'surface' categories are fairly easy to identify and specify, down to the actual physical space they occupy in terms of column inches and as a proportion of the whole. Similar approaches, for example assessing the amount of sexually explicit material in television programmes, or the representation of ethnic minorities, are widely used today. Finer grain analysis of textual material is also possible, as in the use of gender-specific pronouns or other terms.

Classic content analysis is essentially about the analysis of *text* and the more self-evident features of this. *Qualitative* content analysis, as dealt with here, mainly involves transcribed speech and is textual in that sense but quite different from conventional written text. We need to examine some of the differences between spoken and written language before we go any further (see also Chapter 15).

Speaking and writing

People do not speak as they write though it has to be said that there is a kind of formal discourse, as in a lecture, which lies somewhere between the two. But none of us speak like a tightly edited written text: the effect would be inhuman if we did.

Even when the coverage is the same (in a lecture as opposed to a chapter in a book), the spoken version is characterized by various rhetorical devices, for example:

- repetition – bringing the audience back to a key point (in a written version you can turn back to it if necessary);
- elaborative commentary – perhaps a series of 'for instance' anecdotal examples – which give the audience a chance to think on what is being said (in a book you can stop to reflect on what you are reading);
- thinking on your feet – necessary when you are changing gear (fore-warning the audience) or responding to the reaction of the audience (a well-written text anticipates that kind of movement and reactivity and deals with it succinctly).

Now the above applies to an experienced (and presumably, articulate) speaker in a prepared formal setting. An 'unsophisticated' interviewee is in a somewhat different case, but in both instances, in transcription what has been said needs to be reduced to its key points and then these substantive elements put into categories.

Identifying substantive statements

One of the reasons why transcription is such an onerous task is that much of what people say in an interview is redundant in the substantive sense. People vary, of course, and to linguists *no* element of speech is redundant: everything is there for a purpose. But in carrying out the process of transcription you develop a sense of those elements which contribute to the substance of the empirical enquiry, sometimes couched in particularly vivid language. It is difficult to provide an abstract definition of what is substantive and what is not. But, in practice, agreement between different researchers reviewing the same transcript is usually high. The following example (about the use of grievance procedures at work) shows where the substantive statements have been italicized:

> *I'm not a complainer, I'm really not. You don't want to be like that* . . . But . . . well, I got more and more frustrated . . . I mean, you don't want to have to say it . . . *people should understand. You know, being in that position . . . a manager, or whatever.* They should think about it . . . other people. *I tried to show how I felt* . . . not actually saying . . . wouldn't he pick it up? . . . busy or insensitive, I don't know. Months and months . . . and I got, well, frustrated . . . angry. I mean *I like my job and this was spoiling it.* And I thought . . . well, write it down . . . just for myself . . . and when I did . . . well, you could see it then, like *you had a case . . . not just being neurotic.*

Reading this, though you may or may not agree entirely with the selected elements, you can see that they do capture different dimensions of meaning and so could be represented by different category headings.

So there are two stages:

1 identifying substantive statements;
2 deciding on categories.

Neither is a once-and-for-all process: you move back and forth, changing your mind, reviewing and revising while working through different transcripts. This iterative process is the heart of the matter: not linear, rather untidy, but from which emerges an organization of the common meanings derived from different accounts.

Forming categories

As we shall see later, forming categories starts from the analysis of the first transcript. But the reality and robust character of these categories only become apparent as you move from one transcript to another. Here is another practical example – from textile designers' accounts of how they source their design ideas:

> 1 *Buildings – I mean when they're being built . . . incomplete . . . half-built walls and . . . the holes for the windows . . . doors . . .*

scaffolding, that's really exciting. It all has a job to do, functional and ... as you move around it ... it's the perspective ... from an angle you see it. I have a camera with me ... like a visual notebook. When I get an idea I kind of circle round it.

2   *I'm fascinated by stitches. I collect ... old lady type embroidery – boring stuff in a way – and sewing guides – not for the stitches themselves but the kind of patterns they make. Traditional tailors' basting stitches – not neat and finished; they look ... compelling ... so bold and temporary ... but there's a pattern and I try to see how it could work, for me ... Untidy – I mean, I make sketches but I've got all this stuff in boxes and I think – I've got something there – my mind's tidy really.*

3   *Things that belonged to people. My gran's button box: I get them out and I think: if it was bigger, smaller ... and I shuffle them around and I stand back. Sometimes I leave them on a table for days ... and it grows ... and I take photographs and I make sketches – we all do – you work it up from there.*

4   *It's all about scale. In a charity shop, a decoration around the rim of a cup and I think ... if that was much bigger ... round the hem of a skirt ... so I buy the cup and I put in on a shelf and I let it cook ... in my head ... and I do paper overlays, and coloured sketches. It's like a gift: you take it and you make something of it.*

As you read these excerpts through you can see *common* categories that make sense, but also elements that don't conform to this common framework. *How* you name these categories is a creative business in itself: inevitably you will find that sometimes the first heading that comes to mind doesn't really fit, or somehow gets in the way.

Taking the above textile designers' statements, a possible system of categories would be:

- sources of design ideas
- recording/storing of ideas
- transformation and development of ideas.

One essential characteristic of category headings is that they should really *indicate* the character of the statements allocated to them – they should be *descriptive* and not too abstract. Anticipating the writing of the research report you should regard the categories as *sub-headings*, under which to include a representative selection of statements – because there will be a range – with linking commentary from yourself.

One danger in category formation is that of making the categories too narrow (one of the vulnerabilities of qualitative data analysis software because of its extensive storage facilities) so that you end up with a vast number of categories which means, in a sense, you haven't categorized at all. Better to err on the side of breadth (within which you can select a representative range). For example, in the above designers' statements and under the heading of *recording/storing ideas* you could have:

- using a camera as a visual notebook
- collecting material samples
- using sketchbooks
- setting out objects
- making paper overlays.

They're all different but *categorically* they are the same and – important from the perspective of a researcher – the category definition can be justified by inspection of the content.

There is no need to labour the point further; just engaging in the process yourself with your own interview transcripts (or material that the respondents have written for you) will clarify your ideas.

An organizational hierarchy

Think of it like a book: made up of the transcripts organized in 'chapter' headings corresponding to the main questions. Within those chapters you get a range of answers and this is where the creative process of category formation takes place. You've specified the main questions but the actual content is unpredictable.

We have suggested that your initial categories should be *quite* broad – like sub-headings within the 'chapter'. But with broad categories and especially with a large number of transcripts – more than 30, and perhaps fewer that that – your categories will start to bulge. In other words you may need to sub-divide them into sub-sub-headings. But you should first check whether you have made your categories *too* broad so that several statements by the same person are being allocated to the same category: if you're not differentiating enough you are not really analysing the material. Analysis is about making distinctions within your data set so that these differences can be seen more clearly. If the categorical distinctions, when reviewed, are justified, then you have to consider how you will organize and present them and you may be obliged to use data analysis software: this is discussed later (see pp. 146–7), but as it takes time to become fluent in use, this recourse is only justified if your data set is large and so unmanageable by more pedestrian means.

Using the 'book' analogy we can think in terms of an inverted tree diagram (Figure 19.1).

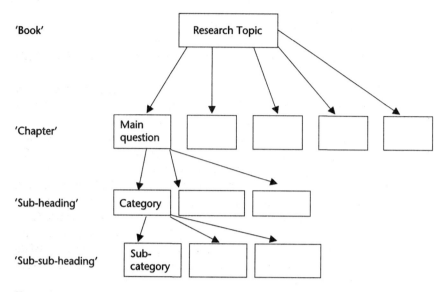

'Book'

'Chapter'

'Sub-heading'

'Sub-sub-heading'

Figure 19.1 Inverted tree diagram of category formation

If this starts to look formidable, remember:

- such an extensive system is only necessary with large data sets (and not always then);
- on the one hand, you shouldn't chop finer than is necessary to make sense of your material – otherwise you *lose* meaning;
- on the other, if you don't chop fine enough you obscure distinctions – a balance has to be struck.

Narrative analysis and categorical analysis

In a narrative interview you don't have a set of pre-determined questions (the 'chapter' headings) although something like this can be derived from the *stage-structure analysis* described on pp. 130–2. Figure 19.1 doesn't exactly apply, but it does in essence. You can still search for main categories and further sub-sections as the meaning of the material dictates. There are no hard-and-fast rules here except the very general rule: how can I analyse the data to make the best presentational and interpretive sense of my material?

Ten-point procedure for analysis

1   Check that the format of your transcripts is easy to work from. This
    requires:
    (a) your questions and interjections in a different typeface from
        the interviewee's: *capitals* for main questions, *italics* for sup-
        plementary questions, prompts and probes.
    (b) at least double-spacing: easier to read and allows you to insert a
        coding (category) reference to the spreadsheet matrix (see p. 143),
        and the highlighted substantive statements.
    (c) each transcript and quotation clearly identified by letter and
        number so that the source of a particular statement can be refer-
        enced: for example A1 would mean interviewee A, category 1.
2   Taking each transcript in turn, go through them highlighting sub-
    stantive statements. When in doubt highlight – you can always delete
    later but if a statement is essentially repeated, circle the one that
    seems fullest or clearest.
3   Don't read transcripts one after another, particularly if they are
    lengthy, otherwise concentration becomes dulled. Depending on
    length, it is a good rule to read through no more than two to three
    transcripts a day but *on successive days*: to give the cumulative process
    a chance to work. This first absorption stage is important, as is coming
    to the readings mentally refreshed. However, if you space the readings
    too far apart you will lose the categories that are forming in your
    mind. It is worth blocking out time (a week or a fortnight) where
    dealing with the transcripts is your only significant (mental) task.
4   After reading through the full set, marking up, go through them again
    but much more quickly:
    (a) checking your highlighted statements – are some redundant?
    (b) scanning those elements you haven't highlighted – are there
        significant statements that have been missed?
5   If possible, get someone else competent to appraise the content, to
    carry out a parallel highlighting exercise. This serves two purposes:
    (a) It provides a simple 'reliability' check – are your selections
        idiosyncratic or arbitrary?
    (b) It obliges you to reconsider areas of disagreement (statements
        they haven't highlighted that you did; statements they have
        which you didn't). You can calculate a simple metric (percentage-
        agreement) but more important is the contribution to the review
        process – making you think again.
6   This is the intellectually creative stage of category formation. Essen-
    tially what you do is go back to the beginning and try to derive a set of

categories for the responses to each question. You do this not for each complete transcript but for each *question*, moving across from one transcript to another. At this point you are just trying to establish a set of categories *not* allocating statements to them – that comes next.

Give these categories headings which are as *descriptive* as possible ('reasons for buying organic produce'; 'sources of stress as a post-graduate research student', and so on). A lot of categories are derived from the first transcript, more from the next but progressively fewer from those that follow because the interviewees are making the same *kind* of points.

Some categories will prove to be redundant, some virtually the same but better phrased, others too broad or abstract but it is important to keep going. At the end of this stage you can look back and see how you've done, ask yourself: *which headings are inadequate or unnecessary?*

7 The categories were derived *from* the statements – not from an *a priori* list – so the statements should more or less fit. Now reverse the process and go through the transcripts again with your list of categories beside you, to check whether each highlighted statement has some-where to go. Mark with a **?** any statements you cannot readily assign to a category.

With your list of **?** statements review category headings to see if they can be modified or added to. Most can be fitted in but some will resist classification. These 'unique' statements may well be important and can be classified simply as that – to be treated in a separate section of the write-up. (The less structured the interview, the more likely this will be.)

8 You need an analysis grid/spreadsheet as in Figure 19.2 (expanded to at least A3 size). Either make it yourself in hardcopy or use *Microsoft Excel* which is straightforward and infinitely extendable. Enter the main question at the top: you will have separate spreadsheets for each question (so that you know to what the categorized answers relate): you give these spreadsheets a lower case prefix (a, b, etc.) which indi-cates which *question* they refer to. You need *two* parallel spreadsheets: one where you enter the actual words of statements (perhaps edited); another where you enter a check mark in each cell where a statement has been inserted.

To begin with, you enter the category headings and number code (along the top); down the side you will be entering the interviewee's name and letter code. You indicate the *question* with a lower case letter, the *respondent* with a capital letter and the *category* with a num-ber (aB7, bC2, and so on), which will locate the reference on the appropriate spreadsheet. Particularly if your categories are broad (and you don't use sub-categories) you may find several qualifying

Question or stage of analysis:

Categories

Interviewees	1	2	3	4	5	6	7	etc.
A								
B								
C								
D								
E								
F								
G								
H								
I								
J								
K								
L								
etc.								

Figure 19.2   Analysis grid/spreadsheet

statements for some respondents: you can locate those by adding a Roman numeral (aB7iii, gC2iv, and so on) but this is not strictly necessary. And if it starts to look too algebraic, remember the earlier caution that such an elaboration may mean your categories are over-inclusive, not differentiating enough.

9 Using the two parallel spreadsheets go through the transcripts putting each substantive statement in its designated category (including those classified as 'unique'). Insert the text on one spreadsheet and a check mark (tick, star or whatever) on the other: the first of these is for qualitative (meaning) analysis; the second for count (frequency) analysis – that is, so many people made a statement (or statements) in this category.

10 As you enter the statements on the spreadsheets, put the *reference* against the statement on the original transcript (bD4, eH14, and so on): that will tell you where it's gone.

High and low inference

The procedural steps described above can seem to gloss over rather a big issue, namely, how do we justify a category we have arrived at? The answer is to reconsider the point made at the very beginning of this chapter: that category formation is a process of interpretation, particularly when dealing with the meanings of what people say rather than more easily verifiable 'objective' phenomena. It is safer not to go too far down the path of inference and keep closer to what is on the surface, as in 'classic' content analysis (pp. 135–6). We need to review the argument.

It's a familiar notion that people may 'mean' the same thing but say it, or express it in their behaviour, in quite different ways. For example, the male of the species is more likely to display anxiety through aggressive behaviour than the female and, within genders, there is considerable variation (psycho-somatic symptoms, hyperactivity, and so on). We are obliged to make inferences if we are to make sense of what people *do*. So it is with what people *say*. If we have derived a category heading 'Dissatisfaction with work conditions' we might include statements like:

> I sometimes think whether you do a good job or not, it makes no difference.

> Well, I had this career review but my Head of Department, he was obviously bored with it, just ticking boxes and scribbling a few words.

> She said: 'Am I supposed to know you?' – a big smile, but she didn't care . . . artificial.

You could construct different category headings: 'Employer–employee relations', 'Problems of inter-personal sensitivity'. You can judge for yourself which heading is more appropriate, but the *latent* content of what goes into the category is clear enough. Essentially the task is to construct categories and definitions (headings) that make sense to other people as a way of organizing and presenting the content of interviews. Such categories are not 'objective' any more than human values are objective, and even where there is a measure of agreement, different people will arrive at rather different categories. The task is to ensure:

- that your categories have been carefully derived and 'make sense';
- that the evidence base is comprehensively presented: the actual statements, as well as the original transcripts and how the interviews were conducted and developed.

People may agree or disagree with your analysis to some extent but they can only do that adequately if they can see where you have come from, and how you substantiate what you have done. But if you don't make inferences you don't make progress in understanding.

Content analysis: a first practical exercise

Like interviewing itself, the practice of content analysis is difficult to learn from a book. And if you have had no prior experience, the procedure described above can seem a daunting task. This is where a simple practical exercise used with my own students (and which can easily be adapted to another context) may be of use:

1   Each student in the group (around eight to twelve in total) is asked to write down on a single sheet of A4 the positive and negative features of the course they are doing.
2   The individual written responses are then photocopied in multiples so that each student has a complete set from the whole group.
3   They then carry out a categorical content analysis, on their own, of the response sheets.

Because the data are written, no transcription is required, and because the points are summary, they are all more or less substantive. But the most difficult task – category derivation and statement allocation – remains. The students then see each other's analysis which brings home to them that, while similar categories tend to be derived, there is no objective, definitive 'correct' set of headings. This is the crucial element of learning about qualitative content analysis: that it is something which can only take place within the operation of the human mind.

Computer-assisted qualitative data analysis software (CAQDAS)

The intellectual burden is one thing but even when that is lifted, and you are perfectly clear as to what you are about, there is an impressive amount of sheer slog involved. Couldn't a computer, using an appropriate form of software do it for you?

To reiterate, computers are unparalleled for:

- storing large amounts of information;
- allowing you to retrieve it according to how it is organized;
- organizing material in ways that can assist understanding and analysis.

At the most simple level you can put your transcripts into the computer, mark up the substantive statements and their related codes, present them in matrix form and also construct tree diagrams (as in Figures 19.1 and 19.2).

But to do that you have to:

1 master the use of the software;
2 buy it (expensive).

There is no market leader in CAQDAS as there is in quantitative data analysis where SPSS (Statistical Program for the Social Sciences) has unchallenged dominance. The nearest is NVivo a development of the earlier NUD*IST Program (Non-numerical Unstructured Data Indexing Searching and Theorizing). You can get a preliminary feel for the software and see whether it might meet your needs by downloading from Scolari's website (http://www. scolari.com).

When and why would you use CAQDAS?

With a modest data set (perhaps fewer than 30 transcripts) it is probably not worth the cost of buying the software and mastering it; *unless* the data are a pilot for a bigger project when you *would* need to use the software and so need to become competent in its use. Otherwise office-standard word-processing software will suffice.

The main problem with CAQDAS is that it can be used unthinkingly and is biased towards a code-and-retrieve style of organization which can lead to fragmentation of the data and the loss of those elements which make for contextual meaning. This is not a *necessary* effect of using the software, rather a tendency built into its construction.

For most lone researchers working on small to medium-scale projects, CAQDAS is not really necessary, but there may be longer-term implications as part of learning the trade of being a social researcher of a qualitative orientation.

The limits of the machine

Computers are the most versatile machines ever produced but they are still machines: they can only be used intelligently by the human mind. A sophisticated camera doesn't make you a photographer: it is the intelligent eye behind it that does that. It is in the area of interpretive judgement that the computer remains very much a machine and where it can fall down (the familiar spell check errors are a function and simple example of this).

But the problem is a little more than this. The hidden operations of computer software may mean that data and data processing are hidden from human sight in the intellectual sense: the convenience of its taking over the donkey-work can limit interpretive sensitivity. For example, I will sometimes analyse quantitative data using no more than a hand calculator for the arithmetical operations because I want to see how the data falls out in the computational process – which affects my understanding (including whether a particular test is sensitive to the raw data). Blind processing can obscure meaning. I recall examining a PhD student and asking her why she'd used a particular test (its suitability was debatable); having allowed SPSS to make the choice for her, she had to say she didn't know.

20 Quantitative analysis of categorical data

Qualitative data – what people say, descriptive material of one kind or another – are not intrinsically numerical in character. Ultimately, of course, *no* data are numerical: measurements of physical phenomena like temperature and air pressure are reflections of more fundamental processes but on a precise interval scale. And the familiar, everyday, measurement of time can seem almost natural: but of course all of these measurement scales are man-made systems related to the physical world.

The applications of number to qualitative data are much more limited and we have to bear these limitations in mind but they are still useful in the sense that they can add something to meaning, not least a level of precision.

Descriptive and inferential statistics

There is a distinction we need to make clear. *Descriptive* statistics – things like averages (known as *means* in statistical science), ranges and frequencies enable you to describe in a tidy, summary format, usually as tables or figures, rather a lot of data. For example, if you have used recording schedules (Chapter 11) with 150 people, you might want to show the frequencies of the different age-ranges in a histogram (Figure 20.1). This distribution would be tedious (and confusing) to describe in words but can be seen almost at a glance.

Inferential statistics are those which enable you to make an inference about differences or relationships between two sets of data. Here we shall deal with two ways of ordering data involving these kinds of statistical analyses: putting data into categories; and putting data into ranks.

Putting categorical data into numerical form

When analysing data into categories for a number of different respondents you can do it in two ways as described in the previous chapter: on one

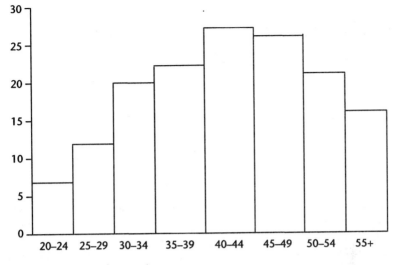

Figure 20.1 Age-range frequencies

spreadsheet you write in what was said; and on the other you put a check mark (this respondent made a statement that fits this category). It is a simple matter to count the check marks and to present a numerical summary of how many people made statements of one kind or another.

But you can also divide up your group (by age or gender, for example) to see whether there are differences in the pattern of what individuals have said. Suppose that in a structured interview PhD students were asked to give their *main* reason for doing a PhD. And suppose their answers could be categorized into either *career development* or *personal development*. For reasons of tidiness we'll assume 100 students were interviewed, with the following results (Table 20.1).

This looks as though older (30+) PhD students are more likely to be determined by reasons of personal development, with younger students more concerned about career implications. In simple numerical terms there *is* a difference, but the numbers are not very large and the question to ask, before

Table 20.1 Reasons for doing a PhD (by age): obtained frequencies

	Career development		Personal development		Totals
Under 30	24	A	16	B	40
30+	22	C	38	D	60
Totals	46		54		N = 100

rushing into erroneous interpretation is: how likely is it that this difference could have occurred by chance? In other words, how *significant* is the difference? Now in probability theory *any* difference could occur by chance. So what we have to consider is the balance of probabilities. This is almost a matter of common sense. It is reasonable to say that if it could have occurred by chance once in a hundred times that is significant; once in a thousand times would be *highly* significant. The lowest level of significance conventionally accepted is one in 20 times by chance (so you wouldn't be *very* confident about that). However, the choice of significance levels depends on (a) sample size; and (b) the type of test employed (see Greene and d'Oliviera 1999). Probabilities are normally expressed as decimal fractions of one: 0.05 (1 in 20); 0.01 (1 in 100), 0.001 (1 in 1000), and so on.

Bearing Table 20.1 in mind we can calculate how the numbers would look if there were no differences between younger and older (30– and 30+) PhD students (Table 20.2). To calculate the *expected* frequencies for each cell (A, B, C, D), we multiply the two relevant marginal totals (those in line) and divide by the total number of subjects (N = 100).

$$\text{Cell A} = \frac{46 \times 40}{100} = 18.4$$

$$\text{Cell B} = \frac{54 \times 40}{100} = 21.6$$

$$\text{Cell C} = \frac{46 \times 60}{100} = 27.6$$

$$\text{Cell D} = \frac{54 \times 60}{100} = 32.4$$

These are the *expected* frequencies if there were no difference at all. Table 20.1 gave the frequencies *actually* obtained. The next step is to calculate the differences between the two (Table 20.3). These are the basic data for computing the statistic known as *chi square* (X^2).

Table 20.2 Expected frequencies if there were no differences between older and younger students

	Career development	Personal development
Under 30	18.4	21.6
30+	27.6	32.4

Table 20.3 Differences between expected and obtained frequencies

	Career development	Personal development
Under 30	−5.6	+5.6
30+	+5.6	−5.6

The computation of chi square

Although quite simple, careful attention is required to the stages of the calculation. First, we *square* each discrepancy in Table 20.3 which gets rid of the signs. This gives us:

31.36	31.36
31.36	31.36

We then *divide* each squared number by the *expected* frequency for that cell (as in Table 20.2). This gives us:

1.70	1.45
1.13	0.97

We then total the results = 5.26, which gives us the value for X^2. What remains?

Calculating degrees of freedom

The kind of categorical table we have here is called a *contingency* table because the numbers in each cell are contingent upon each other. When one cell is fixed in a 2 × 2 table as in our example, *all* the others are fixed. In other words, they only have one *degree of freedom*. The importance of this is that, in order to calculate the significance of chi square from the relevant table, you need to know not just the value of chi square but also the degrees of freedom. In a contingency table with more cells – for example, 3 × 4 – you have to use a simple formula; note that 'degrees of freedom' is abbreviated to *df*:

> df = (r–1) (k–1) where *r* is the number of rows and *k* the number of columns.

In a contingency table that had 3 rows and 4 columns, this would be:

> df = (3–1) (4–1) = 2 × 3 = 6

That doesn't apply to the example we are working out. In our case there is only *one* degree of freedom and, consulting the relevant Table F in Greene and d'Oliviera (1999) we find that 5.25 does not reach the 0.02 level of significance but exceeds by far the 0.03 level. So we can have reasonable confidence that the difference between the two groups of PhD students represents something real. But let's see what follows.

The limitations of chi square

Useful statistic though it is, chi square has some important limitations:

1   If total numbers and the ratio of difference are not large, a significant difference is unlikely. However, if for example we doubled the figures in Table 20.1 but with the same ratio of difference, the result would be highly significant almost reaching the 1 in 1000 (0.001) level.

   In effect, this is no more than the common-sense appreciation that if you find a difference within a large group of people, it is more likely to mean something than if only a modest number of people is involved. But of course, in reality, if you re-run an investigation you may get nothing like the same degree of difference by doubling the numbers of people you interview, showing that the first finding was a fluke. If you *do* find a significant difference, you still have to *explain* it: a statistical test does not do that for you.

2   When the *total* number is less than around 40 in a 2 × 2 table, chi square is less appropriate and with fewer than around 30, it is totally inappropriate (for technical reasons that would not be usefully discussed here). With low numbers the appropriate statistic is Fisher's Test of Exact Probability, but as this involves the computation of *factorials* (written as the number followed by an exclamation mark – 10! for example), you have to use appropriate software – SPSS (Statistical Program for the Social Sciences). The factorial of 10 is $1 \times 2 \times 3 \times 4 \times 5 \times 6 \times 7 \times 8 \times 9 \times 10$ which is a very large number indeed (3,628,800); and the Fisher test involves multiplying the products of these factorials: beyond the scope of the conventional calculator.

3   Directly related to the above, and again for technical reasons, chi square is not recommended for use (at least in a 2 × 2 table) when the *expected* frequency in any cell is less than 10, although a correction can be applied provided no cell is less than 5.

Correlating ranked judgements

In Chapter 13 we described a procedure for interviewing design experts and asking them to rank product samples (textiles in that instance) according to certain criteria. We suggested aesthetic quality, on the one hand, and market appeal, on the other; one can think of other variable criteria such as production feasibility.

In our (fictional) example the textile designers were each asked to rank design samples according to these different criteria from 1 (highest) to 7 (lowest). A useful question to ask is: are the two sets of criteria in agreement even when coming from a different rationale basis? For each expert we would have something like the example given in Table 20.4.

Table 20.4 Ranking of seven textile samples according to aesthetic quality and market appeal

Design	Aesthetic quality	Market appeal
A	4	3.5
B	7	5
C	3	3.5
D	2	1
E	1	2
F	6	7
G	5	6

Note: Designs A and C were seen as equal in market appeal for ranks 3 and 4, so were averaged.

From looking at the ranks we may have the impression that they are in quite close agreement. In order to compute the *level of agreement* we use a test known as Spearman's rank order correlation coefficient (known by the Greek letter *rho*), shown in Table 20.5. This is a 'small sample' or *non-parametric* test, appropriate here with seven pairs of ranks (with larger numbers you would use a so-called *parametric* test).

For each *pair of ranks* we calculate the difference and then square it (d and d^2) and total the sum of squares (written as Σd^2), using the Greek letter *sigma* (sum of).

Table 20.5 Computing Spearman's rho for the data in Table 20.4

d	d^2
0.5	0.25
2.0	4.0
0.5	0.25
1.0	1.0
1.0	1.0
1.0	1.0
1.0	1.0
	$\Sigma d^2 = 8.50$

We then enter the sum of d^2 (Σd^2) into the following formula as well as the total number (7) of textile fabrics which were ranked:

$$\text{rho} = 1 - \frac{6 \times \Sigma d^2}{N^3 - N}$$

$$= 1 - \frac{6 \times 8.5}{7^3 - 7}$$

$$= 1 - \frac{51}{336}$$

$$= 1 - 0.15$$

$$= +0.85$$

So our 'eyeball' impression is largely correct. This is quite a high level of *positive* correlation (note that you can have a *negative* correlation). But the number of ranks is small, so we have to ask the further question: *is this correlation significant?* This can be checked by reference to a table of probabilities for different sample sizes in a standard statistical text (Table H in Greene and d'Oliviera 1999). In this example our finding doesn't quite meet the 0.01 level of significance (0.893) but far exceeds the 0.05 level (0.714) so we can have reasonable confidence that the level of agreement *is* significant.

In our example we would end up with different correlations for each expert: a range of correlations which have to be interpreted.

Averaging ranks: a caution

If there are *separate* panels (groups of experts, consumers or whatever) rating the same products using common criteria, it seems sensible to see how far these different groups agree. You can show this in a graph (descriptive statistics) but can you not also compute the correlation by averaging the ranks? Well, you could but it is not strictly correct because you can only really average numbers that are on an *interval* scale (such as weight, length, height). To take a simple (hypothetical) example which shows the difference between an interval scale and a rank order (or *ordinal*) scale, consider the ranking of seven women in descending order of height (Table 20.6).

The first column shows that the differences in height (on the interval scale) vary between 0.15 metres and 0.05 metres, but in terms of simple rank order the differences are the same. So if you *average* ranks you have to appreciate the limitations of what you are doing.

Table 20.6 Seven women ranked according to actual height (metric) and in rank order

Women	Metric height	Rank order
Anna	2.0 m	1
Beth	1.85 m	2
Charlotte	1.80 m	3
Diana	1.75 m	4
Eva	1.7 m	5
Frances	1.65 m	6
Greta	1.55 m	7

Let us conclude with a hypothetical example where a panel comprised of 10 technical experts and 25 members of the public ranked seven different prototype mobile phones in terms of their preference: putting the most preferred in first place, the least preferred in seventh place, and so on (Table 20.7). We would leave the criteria up to them (although asking them to explain their preferences).

If we carried out the not-quite-legitimate practice of averaging the ranks we might find the following:

Table 20.7 Average ranking of mobile phones by experts and consumers

Model	Experts	Consumers
Z	4.0	3.75
Y	5.75	1.25
X	2.25	3.25
W	1.5	4.5
V	2.75	2.5
U	3.25	5.25
T	6.5	6.25

This is a difficult one to read (averaging ranks inevitably results in decimals) but we still follow the procedure of calculating differences, squaring them and calculating the total (Σd^2) for entering into the formula.

d	d^2
−0.25	0.0625
−4.50	20.25
+1.0	1.0
+3.0	9.0
−0.25	0.0625
+2.0	4.0
−0.25	0.0625
	$\Sigma d^2 = 34.43$

$$\text{rho} = 1 - \frac{6 \times 34.43}{7^3 - 7}$$

$$= 1 - \frac{206.5}{336}$$

$$= 1 - 0.614$$

$$= 0.386$$

Not only is this a very modest correlation, but using the appropriate statistical table we find that for the sample size of seven pairs of ranks the correlation is non-significant. Without this test of significance one might be tempted to claim that there *was* a relationship (albeit modest) between the preferences of experts and consumers. This *interpretive* error, a qualitative judgement, is one where quantitative measures add in a distinctive factor. The correlation does not mean what it appears to show.

Endnote

Quantitative analysis can be complementary in the real sense that it *adds* something to a set of qualitative data. That is, of course, the only justification for using it.

This chapter is an elementary introduction to a vast area. Recommended for reading and reference is the manual by Greene and d'Oliviera, already cited, which is exceptionally clearly written and unalarming for those without prior knowledge of statistics.

21 Writing up interview data

Writing up your data is indivisible from the business of writing a research report as a whole, which takes us straight in to an area of contention.

The formal conventions of research report writing

Learning how to do research is a slow process, and students approach the task with entirely understandable misunderstandings. They will have read, or looked at, large numbers of published research papers with their conventional, standardized structure. The logic of these enables the reader to grasp quite quickly the context, purpose, methods, results and conclusions of the study.

The trouble with these fined down, carefully constructed papers, is that they do not reflect how research actually takes place: the things that an apprentice researcher needs to know and understand if they are to do research themselves. A key question, therefore, is: what is omitted and why?

Obviously a formal report is a tidy account. However, it may be such a tidied-up version of the research project, that not only is it of little help to the would-be researcher but is often an inaccurate account of the investigation: inaccurate by omission at least, because of the pressure coming from the conventions of academic reporting.

The argument for a more naturalistic style of reporting

In the 1960s the distinguished scientist Sir Peter Medawar published an essay (following on from a talk on the BBC Third Programme) entitled 'Is the scientific paper a fraud?' He makes the point that: 'the scientific paper is a fraud in the sense that it does give a totally misleading narrative of the processes of thought that go into the making of scientific discoveries', and castigates the scientific community for being 'ashamed to admit that hypotheses appear in their minds along uncharted by-ways of thought; that they are imaginative and inspirational in character; that they are indeed adventures of the mind' (Medawar 1964: 12).

Although much-cited, Medawar's exhortation appears to have had little effect on practice. However, an empirical study by Gilbert and Mulkay (1988) used the techniques of discourse analysis to compare the formal published papers by a group of specialist biochemists, with their informal accounts of how their scientific discoveries were actually made. They point out that:

> A style is adopted in formal research papers which tends to make the author's personal involvement less visible . . . As a consequence, the findings begin to take on an appearance of objectivity which is significantly different from their more contingent character in informal accounting. This formal appearance is strengthened by the suppression of references to the dependence of experimental observation on theoretical speculation, the degree to which experimenters are committed to specific theoretical positions, and the influence of social relationships on scientists' actions and beliefs, all of which are mentioned frequently in informal accounting.
>
> (1988: 47)

The point is that there are two complementary ways of knowing (or presenting what is known): the logic of a formal paper; and what might be called the 'chronologic' of a narrative report. There is a place for both and a balance to be struck in order that a truer, more complete account is achieved.

This is not to advocate an illogical, undisciplined style of reporting, rather, it is an argument for a style which reflects the actual progress of the researcher *so that the conduct of the research can be appreciated*. A formal 'logical' account is a kind of edited reorganization of the natural sequence of events: and clarifying in its own way.

Having made this contrast apparent, it is important that the distinction is not over-emphasized. The contrast is not black and white but in shades of grey. A narrative is never logically chaotic; nor is a formal paper lacking in narrative structure.

Logic and chronologic: the development of research questions

You cannot sensibly ask questions of an area of research until you know something about it. The exploratory phase may be a little untidy: after all, why did you become interested in the first place? (My own doctoral research into language delay stemmed from the fact that my elder son was, initially, a slow talker though his understanding was quite advanced.) So a spirit of curiosity is the starting point and from that, as you become better informed, research questions emerge (in my case, what is the relationship between speech comprehension and production in young children?).

But even when you have done a lot of preparatory work – reading the literature, talking to colleagues, and so on – your research questions continue to develop.

The *logic* is that you first formulate your questions and then develop methods to answer them. In fact, what happens is that as you get into your empirical enquiry, you find you need to modify, or add to, your original questions (in the example given: why is there a time-lag between *understanding* vocabulary and *using* it, when speech capability is there?).

Acknowledging the process of discovery

If you have conducted interviews as a researcher, you've done so to answer research questions. (NB The broad questions of your research, not the actual questions you ask in the interview.) But in the emergent character of naturalistic research, you are continually modifying those questions. In carrying out the interviews, analysing them and, even in the later stage of writing up the results of your analysis, you can come to see that you are answering at least slightly different research questions from the ones you formulated at an earlier stage. You modify your research, of course, but you may also adapt your questions to better fit the character of what you are researching. There's nothing corrupt about this: it happens all the time – it just isn't formally recorded because it violates the conventions of 'logical' structure.

This process of discovery is continuous as you focus on your data collection and analysis. Writing up is the ultimate close encounter: but it is a closeness (attention to precise detail) where you are also standing back to get everything in the frame, to see your data in their entirety.

Writing as discovery

Writing a research report is an act of reconstruction and of intellectual discovery. What can be left to be discovered? After all, you are familiar with all the elements, have checked and inspected them perhaps dozens of times.

But in social research, particularly that of a qualitative character, the real discoveries are not of startling new facts (there aren't many of those) but *conceptual*: seeing familiar aspects of our social world differently, making sense of it in an original way.

When you get down to the business of writing up your research – putting the whole thing together – you are comprehensively *constructing* it for the first time. And in so doing you discover your extended understanding of it. It has been argued that you don't know what you think until you write it down. I would add: you *discover* what you think by writing it down.

Weaving a narrative

Organization is a process of interaction: your interview data organized on spreadsheets (the source for writing up) and a mind organized by the very process of displaying your material. Whether you've done your analysis as a set of categories within the answers to a main question, in a semi-structured or other kind of interview, or as a stage-structure analysis of a 'narrative' interview, you will still *in essence* be telling the story of what you've found.

Your spreadsheets will be in the developmental order of your main questions or the stages you've identified: like chapter or section headings. Your categories, or the range of elements in each stage, may contribute sub-headings.

The essential character of writing up interview data is to weave a narrative which is interpolated with illustrative quotations. In this way you are allowing the interviewees to speak for themselves, with linking material which is mainly there to ensure continuity and point up the significance of what they are saying. John and Elizabeth Newson were pioneers of this style of reporting interview data. Their (1963) book *Infant Care in an Urban Community* remains a vivid demonstration of its potency. A more recent example is the study by Burghes and Brown (1995) of single lone mothers. An extended quotation from their research which exemplifies what is being advocated is given in the box.

Other sources of help mentioned by the single lone mothers included a local family centre, a foster mother and other mothers living in the same hostel:

'I was quite lucky . . . even though I didn't have support from my family . . . I were in a hostel for young mothers when I first had J . . . we all rallied round together . . . they helped me a lot . . . told me about their experiences about bringing up a baby'.

Four mothers also referred specifically to help from their boyfriends' mothers, while two cited support received from their boyfriends themselves. Grandparents and friends were also mentioned, sometimes as part of the assistance received from an extended family consortium:

'. . . his sister . . . used to come over and talk to me. She used to stay in the house with me till him or his mum came back from work so it weren't so bad . . . she either watches him or me mum watches him or S watches him when I go out'.

'. . . I had all my friends and they helped me . . . My mum, my auntie and then my cousins would come and take him out and things like that'.

'I was living with a full family so there was a lot of help there. So it'd probably be a totally different story if I was on my own'.

Sometimes, however, support from extended family and friends have not lasted beyond an initial burst of enthusiasm following the birth:

'. . . for the first six months of having her it was fine . . . people were very willing to babysit for a new baby; but then when it got to the teething stage, the friends disappeared'.

'. . . When I had her I had a lot of help but now she's one . . . they don't want to know. And it seems harder for me all the time'.

Notice these things:

- the balance of quotation and inserted text (discussed further below);
- the unobtrusive nature of these insertions;
- the vivid quality of the quotations;
- that the authors have been careful to indicate the range and variety of the answers.

Integrating quantitative analysis

Special applications of quantitative data analysis were discussed in Chapter 20 but there is a more routine use of numerical data which is essentially *displaying* the balance of categorized statements in simple count form as a table. These can be interpolated in the narrative to show how many of the interviewees made that point (or one like it) or how many made different or contradictory points. Sometimes it is adequate to do this alongside a simple set of quotations as in Burghes and Brown's account of help received from boyfriends' mothers. But anything more than that is probably best presented in a table. Look at Table 21.1 (hypothetical data).

The balance of reasons for leaving a previous job would be rather complicated to describe in words, but as set out in the table the findings can be seen at a glance. How *significant* the apparent differences are is another matter but this can still be woven into the narrative (you don't need to show all the working out, just the result).

Table 21.1 Reasons given for leaving last employment by gender

	Unsatisfactory pay	Unsatisfactory social relationships	Unsatisfactory career prospects
M (N = 17)	8	4	5
F (N = 20)	4	10	6

The balance of selected quotations

Balance here means that within the range of quotations (selected from the spreadsheet analysis) the excerpts should be *representative* of the total range.

Achieving a balance within the selected quotations is no easy matter. The basic rule is that you should guard against selecting those quotations that fit *your* preferences or which present a neater picture than the reality. The kind of misrepresentations which are carefully constructed from what people did actually say are the most difficult to deal with. However, the same unbalanced result can arise from an entirely innocent process where there is a kind of 'drift' in those quotations that catch your attention so that others are less regarded: this is part of the half-unconscious process of construction. How can one guard against it? It is a matter of disciplined review of your progressive selection:

1 As you select quotations from your spreadsheets you should highlight them. That tells you which ones have been chosen and which ones have not.
2 You maintain an *audit trail*:
   (a) original transcripts with substantive statements highlighted
   (b) categorized spreadsheets with selected quotations for inclusion in the write-up highlighted
   (c) the written report.
   If you do this carefully, it will act as an automatic check *for yourself* at each stage of the process.
3 Periodically, as you write you should scrutinize your spreadsheets to check the justification for your choice: is it really representative? Some quotations exactly capture the general picture; but there may be nuances and emphases which can be overlooked.

The balance between quotation and linking narrative

The first principle here is that linking material should not take over and swamp the verbatim excerpts. This is partly a matter of simple metric: how much of each? The answer depends on the material and purposes of the research but a rule-of-thumb guide is that quotations should be not *less* than one-third and not *more* than two-thirds of the total. The excerpt from Burghes and Brown's study is at the higher end of this range, and it does speak for itself.

The second principle is that, within a particular sector or category, in dealing with a particular topic, the *number* of quotations is part of the impact of quality. Sometimes you would want to convey the force of people's feelings by giving several quotations that do say essentially the same thing: it drives the point home.

Similarly, in a complex topic with no straightforward representative quotations, you will need to reconstruct the complex picture, the shades of opinion, with a variable range of quotations. In an understandable desire to 'make sense' of the material it is easy to oversimplify. After all, these statements were identified originally as having 'something to say'.

The aim is to represent what the people you interviewed told you, in response not just to the questions you asked them, but the *purposes* of the research. It is necessary to keep that larger frame in mind in your analysis and writing up. Research interviews are not simply a vehicle for interesting conversations.

22 Combining interview data with data from other sources

Interviews provide not just one *source* of data but one kind of data. And the relationship between that and other kinds of evidence is not necessarily straightforward.

What is sometimes known as *post-modern* interviewing (Gubrium and Holstein 2003) takes the position that positivist notions of reliability and validity and 'triangulation' misconstrue the nature of what is constructed by interviewees in giving an account of themselves. The validity of such accounts is intrinsic: it doesn't have to be 'checked out'. An appreciation of this *con-structivist* perspective is a matter of contention. But constructivist or not, there is a theoretical challenge as to the purpose of people's accounts of themselves.

A starting point is to examine the notion of 'triangulation'.

Triangulation in practice

This term is much bandied about by those who have some notion that it involves getting more than one 'fix' on something to locate or confirm it more precisely and accurately. The term has its main (and original) application in surveying, particularly for map-making: a pattern of triangles, covering the whole country, marked at each angle by a trigonometric point (or *trig point*). In open country this is indicated by a concrete construction rather like the base of a sundial; in cities usually it will be marked by a vertical arrow on the side of a wall. Imaginary lines between these points locate features within the triangles. But of course, in moving from one point to another we are dealing with phenomena which are of the same kind: distance, altitude, angles, and so on.

When the notion of triangulation is applied to human data, it is soon apparent in moving from one fix – for example, what people say about themselves – to other fixation points such as what they do, or what records show, that we are not working in the same dimensions: the 'triangulation' bearings locate something more or less different each time.

This is a theoretical problem (one that requires explanation): it does not necessarily mean that one source of data is wrong or in error. The error may lie in our assumptions: we should not expect different *kinds* of data to simply agree, or even act as some qualification. The relationship is more complex.

Words and deeds: knowledge and behaviour

Even if we accept that an interview, at least in terms of feelings, attitudes, understandings and perceptions, provides access to a person's subjective world – a self-construction – the question remains as to why they 'construct' themselves as they do. An interview will often include some kind of confronting of these personal worlds (see pp. 35–6 on 'reflecting'). A psychotherapist who viewed such constructs as a form of defence against self-knowledge might be much more challenging.

But there remains the question of the relationship between what people express in words and the counterpart of these as manifested in behaviour. For example, a person may express racist views, or racial tolerance, *verbally* but *behave* in the opposite way. Other presumed links are more straightforward: people may make statements about what they do – but are these statements confirmed by observation?

In a different way this 'discrepancy' is apparent in what people *know* (about health risks, for example) and the behavioural habits they display. There can be no-one who is unaware of the health risks of smoking: this influences the behaviour of some people, but not that of a majority of smokers. It could be argued that they are making an 'informed choice' but this rational model of human psychology does not apply. The simple fact is that people often find they cannot change their behaviour even when they want to: there is no real choice involved. Programmes of drug education and sex education are based on a similar fallacy which misunderstands the relationship between rationality and behaviour.

Interview data have to be taken as 'valid' in their own right: they add something different to other data. We need to think not so much in terms of triangulation or cross-checking as of the complementary role of different kinds of data.

Interviews as a complement to survey data

Survey data are usually large-scale, and representative of the group to which they relate: prisoners on parole; patients returned home after day surgery; students who have dropped out of university; women who have had their first baby after the age of 40, and so on, depending on the area of research interest.

For these groups there are available national level statistics: in the UK from the Office of National Statistics or Government Departments like the Home Office (often very helpful to *bona fide* researchers). Here the research purpose of interviews is quite simple: what is it like to have passed through this experience? In effect, what lies behind the statistics? This is exactly what Burghes and Brown did in the study cited in the previous chapter: the framework was provided by national statistics on teenage lone mothers. They only actually interviewed 30, yet the vivid quality of the interviews, and the careful analysis justify this as a technique to illuminate the statistical context.

Interviews combined with questionnaire survey data

Questionnaires are usually best employed as a survey technique to gather relatively straightforward factual data in response to closed questions, for example within a defined occupational group (ceramic designers, trainee solicitors, staff in a call centre). This provides 'bare bones' data on to which you have to put some flesh.

As with any summary information, a pattern may be apparent which can only be satisfactorily explored by some kind of interview technique (whatever is feasible and appropriate). For example, ceramic designers may have flagged up the lack of school provision in their subject area; trainee solicitors the difficulty of getting a training contract; call-centre staff, a lack of back-up from management in dealing with some queries from customers. From which a next stage is to ask individuals to tell you more about it, and explore the answers.

It is quite common to include a section in a postal questionnaire asking for volunteers to take part in a follow-up interview. A questionnaire survey plus 30 interviews (or thereabouts) makes for a substantial piece of research.

Interviews combined with participant observation

As noted in Chapter 6, the detailed observation of people's behaviour in a 'natural' setting has an apparently irresistible validity and we noted the need for thorough and comprehensive recording. But the human eye is not a camera: it does not just record but selects and *interprets*. The meaning of behaviour is not self-evident: motives are the hidden dimensions. And while observation (of social interactions, for example) will provide clues, *asking* people questions relating to what you've observed (perhaps obliquely, the purpose of widely framed open questions) will guide your interpretation.

Interviews as part of case studies

Case studies as a research method tend to be misunderstood and correspondingly devalued. At a common-sense level the term is often used to cite an example in the form of an expanded anecdote – what might be called a 'vignette' – a glimpse of someone's 'case'.

However, a research case study is wider in its application and aims to investigate a social phenomenon (individual, group, institution, profession) in its contemporary context, and does so by looking for *multiple* forms of evidence including:

- observation (participant or detached);
- collection of documents and records (minutes of meetings, letters received and sent, summary statistical data routinely recorded, and so on);
- the collation of 'artefacts' (things made, work samples of one kind or another);
- interviews in various forms, as described in this book.

The task is to build up a comprehensive picture from such varied elements. For example, if you were investigating literacy standards in a primary school you might:

- observe reading sessions and reading-related teaching;
- collect curriculum statements, details of in-school library initiatives, lists of reading schemes and other materials employed, national test results, and so on;
- take samples of children's unaided written work;
- carry out interviews with teachers, parents and children.

All the elements are different but complementary, and one can see that the interviews may qualify and interpret the findings from the other data sources.

Data collection in real-life settings

The real world is not organized for researchers: data will be incomplete, difficult to access, problematic to interpret *particularly when considered in isolation.* There will, inevitably, be elements of contradiction: in the above example perhaps between expressed policy, actual practice, the views of teachers and parents (and children).

People have a great deal to tell us: appreciating this means attempting to enter someone else's world – the world as they see it. Marcus Aurelius made that point exactly. This effort of empathetic understanding aims to capture the interviewee's perspective and relate this to the other elements that make up social reality for them.

Real-world research is not only untidy and complicated: it constitutes a theoretical challenge, namely, how to make sense of what may appear to be discrepant or discordant elements. Therein lies the fascination of this style of research.

References

Benedikt, M. (1992) Cyberspace: some proposals. In *Cyberspace: First Steps.* Cambridge, MA: MIT Press.

Blackburn, S. (1994) *Oxford Dictionary of Philosophy.* Oxford: Oxford University Press.

Bourque, L. and Fielder, E.P. (2002) *How to Conduct Telephone Surveys.* London: Sage.

Brewer, J. and Hunter, A. (1989) *Multi-method Research.* London: Sage.

Bruner, J.S. (1987) Life as narrative, *Social Research*, 54: 11–32.

Burgess, R.G. (1983) *Inside Comprehensive Education: A Study of Bishop McGregor School.* London: Methuen.

Burghes, L. and Brown, M. (1995) *Single Lone Mothers: Problems, Prospects and Policies.* London: Family Policy Studies Centre.

Derrida, J. (1976) *Of Grammatology.* Baltimore, MD: Johns Hopkins Press.

Deutscher, I. (1966) Words and deeds: social science and social policy, *Social Problems*, 235–54.

Ditton, J. (1977) *Part-time Crime: An Ethnography of Fiddling and Pilferage.* London: Macmillan.

Frey, J.H. and Oishi, S.M. (1995) *How to Conduct Interviews by Telephone and in Person.* London: Sage.

Gaskell, G. (2000) Individual and group interviewing, in M.W. Bauer and G. Gaskell (eds), *Qualitative Researching with Text, Image and Sound.* London: Sage.

Gaskell, G. and Bauer, M.W. (2000) Towards public accountability: beyond sampling, reliability and validity, in M.W. Bauer and G. Gaskell (eds), *Qualitative Researching with Text, Image and Sound.* London: Sage.

Gilbert, G.N. and Mulkay, M. (1988) *Opening Pandora's Box: A Sociological Analysis of Scientists' Discourse.* Cambridge: Cambridge University Press.

Gill, R. (2000) Discourse analysis, in M.W. Bauer and G. Gaskell (eds), *Qualitative Researching with Text, Image and Sound.* London: Sage.

Gillham, B. (2000a) *Developing a Questionnaire.* London: Continuum.

Gillham, B. (2000b) *Case Study Research Methods.* London: Continuum.

Gillham, B. (2000c) *The Research Interview.* London: Continuum.

Grau, O. (2003) *Virtual Art from Illusion to Immersion.* Cambridge, MA: MIT Press.

Green, R. (2004) *Internet Art.* London: Thames and Hudson.

Greene, J. and d'Oliviera, M. (1999) *Learning to Use Statistical Tests in Psychology.* Buckingham: Open University Press.

Gubrium, J.F. and Holstein, J.A. (eds) (2003) *Post-modern Interviewing.* London: Sage.

Hart, C. (1998) *Doing a Literature Review.* London: Sage.

Holdaway, S. (1983) *Inside the British Police: A Force at Work*. Oxford: Blackwell.

Jochelovitch, S. and Bauer, M.W. (2000) Narrative interviewing, in M.W. Bauer and G. Gaskell (eds), *Qualitative Researching with Text, Image and Sound*. London: Sage.

Lincoln, Y. S. and Guba, E.G. (1985) *Naturalistic Inquiry*. London: Sage.

Lowndes, S. (2003) *Social Sculpture: Art, Performance and Music in Glasgow*. Glasgow: Stopstop.

Medawar, P.B. (1964) Is the scientific paper a fraud? In D. Edge (ed.), *Experiment*. London: BBC.

Morecambe, G. and Sterling, M. (2002) *Cary Grant: In Name Only*. London: Robson Books.

Moser, C.A. and Kalton, G. (1986) *Survey Methods in Social Investigation*. Aldershot: Gower Publishing.

Myers, G. (2000) Analysis of conversation and talk, in M.W. Bauer and G. Gaskell (eds), *Qualitative Interviewing with Text, Image and Sound*. London: Sage.

Nash, C.L. and West, D.J. (1985) Sexual molestation of young girls: a retrospective survey, in D.J. West (ed.), *Sexual Victimisation*. Aldershot: Gower Publishing.

Newson, J. and Newson, E. (1963) *Infant Care in an Urban Community*. London: Allen & Unwin.

Patrick, J. (1973) *A Glasgow Gang Observed*. London: Eyre-Methuen.

Polkinghorne, D. (1988) *Narrative Knowing and the Human Sciences*. Albany, NY: SUNY Press.

Robson, C. (2002) *Real World Research*, 2nd edn. Oxford: Blackwell.

Russell, D.E.H. (1983) The incidence and prevalence of intrafamilial and extra-familial sexual abuse of female children, *Child Abuse and Neglect*, 7: 133–46.

Taylor, A. (1993) *Women Drug Users: An Ethnography of an Injecting Community*. Oxford: Clarendon Press.

Truss, L. (2003) *Eats, Shoots and Leaves*. London: Profile Books.

Whyte, W. F. (1955) *Street Corner Society*, 2nd edn. Chicago: University of Chicago Press.

Wittgenstein, L. (1973) *Tractatus Logico-Philosophicus*. Cambridge: Cambridge University Press.

Yin, R. K. (2002) *Case Study Research*, 3rd edn. London: Sage.

Index